✧   *Companions for the Journey*   ✧

Praying with
Julian of Norwich

✧ *Companions for the Journey* ✧

Praying with
Julian of Norwich

by Gloria Durka

Saint Mary's Press
Christian Brothers Publications
Winona, Minnesota

✧ *For Paul* ✧

Those who are wise shall shine
like the brightness of the firmament;
and those who turn many to righteousness,
like the stars forever and ever.
(Daniel 12:3, RSV)

The publishing team for this publication included Carl Koch, FSC, development editor; Rita Rae Kramer, manuscript editor; Lynn Dahdal, typesetter; Richard Hultman, cover designer; and Elaine Kohner, illustrator.

The acknowledgments continue on page 105.

Printed in the United States of America

Printing: 6 5 4 3 2

Year: 1995 94 93 92 91 90 89

ISBN 0-88489-221-2

✧ Contents ✧

Foreword   7

Preface   13

Introduction   15

Meditations

1. God Is Our Mother   24
2. Why We Should Pray   29
3. True Spirituality   35
4. We Are Fastened on God   40
5. God Alone Suffices   46
6. We All Need to Be Loved and to Love   51
7. Nothing Can Separate Us from God's Love   57
8. Courage   62
9. Trust in Our Giftedness   67
10. Recognizing Goodness   72
11. Compassion   77
12. We Are God's Work of Art   82
13. Hope   88
14. Trusting Prayer When God Seems Absent   94
15. All Shall Be Well   99

For Further Reading   107

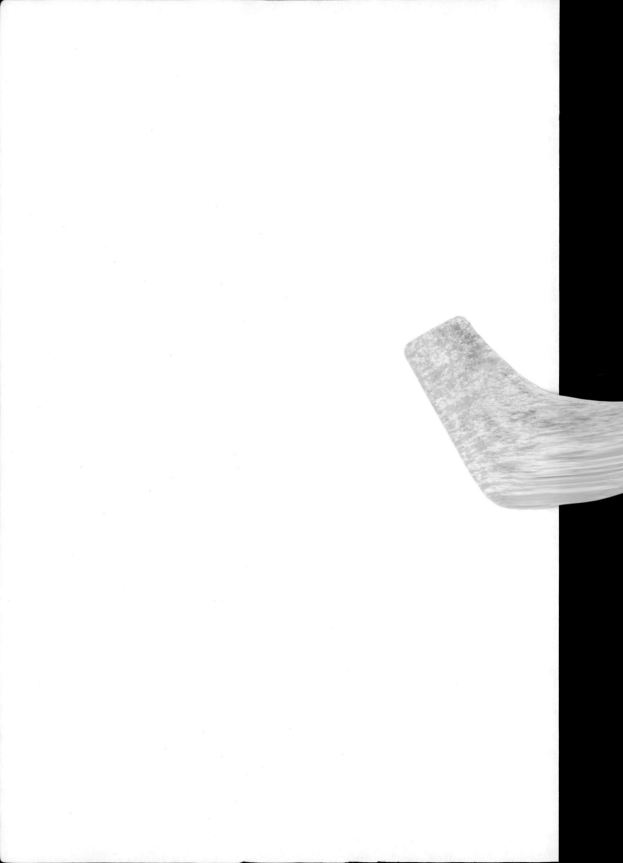

✧ Foreword ✧

Companions for the Journey

Just as food is required for human life, so are companions. Indeed, the word *companions* comes from two Latin words: *com,* meaning "with," and *panis,* meaning "bread." Companions nourish our heart, mind, soul, and body. They are also the people with whom we can celebrate the sharing of bread.

Perhaps the most touching stories in the Bible are about companionship: the Last Supper, the wedding feast at Cana, the sharing of the loaves and the fishes, and Jesus breaking bread with the disciples on the road to Emmaus. Each incident of companionship with Jesus revealed more about his mercy, love, wisdom, suffering, and hope. When Jesus went to pray on the Mount of Olives, he craved the companionship of the Apostles. They let him down. But God sent the Spirit to inflame the hearts of the Apostles, and they became faithful companions to Jesus and to each other.

Throughout history, other faithful companions have followed Jesus and the Apostles. These saints and mystics have also taken the journey from conversion, through suffering, to resurrection. Just as they were inspired by the holy people who went before them, so too may you take them as your companions as you walk on your spiritual journey.

The Companions for the Journey series is a response to the spiritual hunger of Christians. This series makes available the rich spiritual teachings of mystics and guides whose wisdom can help us on our pilgrimage. As you complete the last meditation in each volume, it is hoped that you will feel supported, challenged, and affirmed by a soul-companion on your spiritual journey.

The spiritual hunger that has emerged over the last twenty years is a great sign of renewal in Christian life. People fill retreat programs and workshops on topics in spirituality. The demand for spiritual directors exceeds the number available. Interest in the lives and writings of saints and mystics is increasing as people search for models of whole and holy Christian life.

Praying with the Saints

Praying with Julian of Norwich is more than just a book about Julian's spirituality. This book seeks to engage you in praying in the way that Julian did about issues and themes that were central to her experience. Each meditation can enlighten your understanding of her revelations and lead you to reflect on your own experience.

The goal of *Praying with Julian of Norwich* is that you will discover her wonderfully alive spirituality and integrate her spirit and wisdom into your relationship with God, with your sisters and brothers, and with your own heart and mind.

Suggestions for Praying with Julian

Meet Julian, a caring companion for your pilgrimage, by reading the Introduction, which begins on page 15. It provides a brief biography of Julian and an outline of the culture in which she lived. The major themes of her spirituality are also highlighted.

Once you meet Julian, you will be ready to pray with her and to encounter God, nature, other Christians, and yourself in new and wonderful ways. To help your prayer, here are some suggestions that have been part of the tradition of Christian spirituality:

Create a sacred space. Jesus said, "When you pray, go to your private room, shut yourself in, and so pray to your God who is in that secret place, and your God who sees all that is done in secret will reward you" (Matthew 6:5–6). Solitary prayer is best done in a place where you can have privacy and silence, both of which can be luxuries in the lives of busy people. If privacy and silence are not possible, create a quiet, safe place within yourself, perhaps while riding to and from work, while sitting in line at the dentist's office, or while waiting for someone. Do the best you can, knowing that a loving God is present everywhere. Whether the meditations in this book are used for solitary prayer or with a group, try to create a prayerful mood with candles, meditative music, and a cross.

Open yourself to the power of prayer. Every human experience has a religious dimension. All of life is suffused with God's presence. So remind yourself that God is present as you begin your period of prayer. Do not worry about distractions. If something keeps intruding during your prayer, spend some time talking with God about it. Be flexible—because God's Spirit goes where God wills it.

Prayer can open your mind and widen your vision. Be open to new ways of seeing God, people, and yourself. As you open yourself to the Spirit of God, different emotions are evoked, such as sadness from tender memories, or joy from a celebration recalled. Our emotions are messages from God that can tell us much about our spiritual quest. Also, prayer strengthens our will to act. Through prayer, God can touch our will and empower us to live according to what we know is true.

Finally, many of the meditations in this book will call you to employ your memories, your imagination, and the circumstances of your life as subjects for prayer. The great mystics and saints realized that they had to use all of their resources to know God better. Indeed, God speaks to us continually and touches us constantly. We must learn to listen and feel with all the means that God gave us.

Come to prayer with an open mind, heart, and will.

Preview each meditation before beginning. Spend a few moments previewing the readings and especially the reflection activities. Several reflection activities are given in each meditation because different styles of prayer appeal to different personalities or personal needs. **Note that each meditation has more reflection activities than can be done during one prayer period. Therefore, select only one or two reflection activities each time you use a meditation. Do not feel compelled to complete all of the reflection activities.**

Read meditatively. After you have placed yourself in God's presence, the meditations offer you a story about Julian and a reading from her writings. Take your time reading. If a particular phrase touches you, stay with it. Relish its feelings, meanings, and concerns.

Use the reflections. Following the readings is a short reflection in commentary form that is meant to give perspective to the readings. Then you will be offered several ways of meditating on the readings and on the theme of the prayer. You may be familiar with the different methods of meditating, but in case you are not, they are described briefly here:

✦ *Repeated short prayer or mantra:* One means of focusing your prayer is to use a *mantra*, or prayer word. The mantra may be a single word or a short phrase taken from the readings or from the Scriptures. For example, a mantra for a meditation on courage might be "I go before you" or "trust." Repeated slowly in harmony with your breathing, the mantra helps you center your heart and mind on one action or attribute of God.

✦ *Lectio divina:* This type of meditation is "divine studying," a concentrated reflection on the word of God or the wisdom of a spiritual writer. Most often in *lectio divina* you will be invited to read one of the passages several times and then concentrate on one or two sentences, pondering their meaning for you and their effect on you. *Lectio divina* commonly ends with formulation of a resolution.

✦ *Guided meditation:* In this type of meditation, our imagination helps us consider alternative actions and likely consequences. Imagination helps us experience new ways of seeing God, our neighbors, ourselves, and nature. When Jesus told his followers parables and stories, he engaged their imagination. Several times in this book you will be asked to follow a guided meditation.

One way of beginning a guided meditation is to read the scene or story several times until you know the outline and can recall it when you enter into reflection. Or prior to your prayer time, you may wish to record the meditation on a tape recorder. If so, remember to allow pauses for reflection between phrases and to speak with a slow, peaceful pace and tone. Then during prayer, when you have finished the readings and the reflection commentary, you can turn on your recording of the meditation and be led through it. If you find your own voice too distracting, ask a friend to make the tape for you.

✦ *Examen of consciousness:* The reflections often will ask you to examine how God has been speaking to you in your past and present experience—in other words, the reflections will ask you to examine your awareness of God's presence in your life.

✦ *Journal writing:* Writing is a process of discovery. If you write for any length of time, stating honestly what is on your mind and in your heart, you will unearth much about who you are, how you stand with your God, what deep longings reside in your soul, and more. In some instances you may be asked to write a dialog with Jesus or someone else. If you have never used writing as a means of meditation, try it. Reserve a special notebook for your journal writing. If desired, you can go back to your journal entries at a future time for an examen of consciousness.

✦ *Action:* Occasionally, a reflection may suggest singing a favorite hymn, going for a walk, or undertaking some other physical activity. Actions can be meaningful forms of prayer.

Using the Meditations for Group Prayer

If you wish to use the meditations for community prayer, these suggestions may be of help:

✦ Read the theme to the group. Call the group into the presence of God, using the short opening prayer. Invite one or two participants to read one or both of the readings. If you use both readings, observe the pause between them.

✦ The reflection commentary may be used as a reading, or it can be deleted, depending on the needs and interests of the group.

✦ Select one of the reflection activities for your group. Allow sufficient time for your group to reflect, to do a centering prayer or mantra, to accomplish a studying prayer (*lectio divina*), or to finish an examen of consciousness. Depending on the group and the amount of available time, you may want to invite the participants to share their reflections, responses, or petitions with the group.

✦ Reading the passage from the Scriptures may serve as a summary of the meditation.

✦ If a formulated prayer or a psalm is given as a closing, it may be recited by the entire group. Or you may ask participants to offer their own prayers for the closing.

Now you are ready to begin praying with Julian of Norwich, a delightful companion on this stage of your spiritual journey. For many years, Julian has been a welcome guide and supportive friend for people seeking a closer relationship with God. It is hoped that you will find her to be a true soul-companion.

CARL KOCH, FSC
Editor

✧ Preface ✧

Julian of Norwich

The following pages start you on a journey into the spirituality of Julian of Norwich. I am convinced that once you have had a taste of her wisdom, you will be enticed to read and pray over her book *Showings* in its entirety. My experience has taught me that every pilgrimage into Julian's life and work or to her anchorhold in Norwich, England, is filled with pleasant surprises. The nature of a pilgrimage is such that transformation occurs not at the end of the trip but in the making of the journey. Dame Julian's theology and spirituality make the journey worth the trip. I hope that through this modest work you will share Julian's joy in God's amazing love for all of us.

GLORIA DURKA
Feast of Dame Julian of Norwich
8 May 1988

✧ Introduction ✧

Julian's Life

Almost nothing is known about Julian's life except what she wrote about herself and her calling as an anchoress. We do not even know her real name. As was the custom of anchoresses, she took the name Julian from the name of the church to which she was attached—Saint Julian's.

Julian was born in Norwich, England, in 1342. Most likely she was schooled at the Benedictine convent at Carrow. She called herself unlettered, which probably meant that she did not have higher education as we know it. That Julian was educated at all indicates that she was from an upper-class family, possibly from the increasingly affluent group of Norwich merchants and professionals.

In several places in her writings, Julian protested her ignorance, but this was a well-known rhetorical device often used in appealing for the reader's benevolence. Julian had mastered literary skills better than most of her contemporaries had. Besides being competent in English, as an upper-class person she probably spoke and read French. Many ideas that were current on the Continent show up in her theories, suggesting that she had access to manuscripts circulating from the rest of Europe.

The Showings

During a serious illness at age thirty, as we learn from her own account, Julian received sixteen dramatic revelations of the love of God. She called these revelations "showings." Julian recorded the presence of her mother and the arrival of a parson to administer the last rites. They and Julian presumed that she was dying. The presence of her mother and a parish priest at her bedside suggests that she had not joined a cloistered religious community at the time of her showings.

Nothing in her writings suggests that Julian was committed to the observances of a religious order, although some historians have concluded that Julian became a Benedictine nun. While this is not certain, it is likely. Saint Julian's Church belonged to the Benedictine nuns at Carrow; therefore it is natural to suppose that Julian had some relationship with the convent.

Very likely—though it cannot be proved—the impression made by her revelations was what, most of all, impelled Julian to become an anchoress.

The Wise Anchoress

The solitary vocation of an anchoress was not unusual in medieval times. Records show that Norwich had well over fifty solitaries between the time of Julian's birth in the fourteenth century and the coming of the Protestant Reformation in the sixteenth century. To become an anchoress, a candidate had to satisfy the bishop that she had a genuine sense of God's calling and an adequate means of support. After the celebration of a special mass, the new anchoress was solemnly conducted to her anchorhold, a small room often built into the wall of a church, where she would live the rest of her life. Julian's anchorhold was in Saint Julian's of Norwich.

As an anchoress Julian was, in effect, a hermit. She withdrew from society in order to devote herself completely to prayer and contemplation. She could see the altar and receive Communion through an opening in the church's wall. Even though she withdrew from society, Julian's counsel was sought by many people. Counseling other Christians was a common feature in the life of a hermit.

Julian lived a long life, but the exact date of her death is not known. In a will made in 1416, a citizen of Norwich made

Julian his beneficiary. So we can presume that she was still alive in 1416, when she would have been seventy-four. Reaching such an age was a feat remarkable in itself when we consider that England experienced three outbreaks of bubonic plague during Julian's lifetime.

The period of time during which Julian lived was tumultuous. Testifying to great disharmony in the Church, the popes, under pressure, abandoned Rome and resided in Avignon, France, from 1309 to 1377. Then the Great Schism in the Church began in 1378 and lasted nearly forty years. At one point during the Schism, three rivals laid claim to the papacy.

From 1337 to 1453, England and France fought the on-again, off-again Hundred Years' War. Closer to home, Julian knew of the ravages of the Peasants' Revolt of 1381. During these agrarian uprisings, especially in East Anglia, Bishop Henry Despenser of Norwich took the lead in suppressing the revolt. Norwich castle was captured for a time by a rebel leader who was later caught and executed by the bishop's troops. King Richard II was deposed in 1399, and two other kings (Henry IV and Henry V) followed by the time of Julian's death. Julian was apprised of these national dramas by the merchants and peasants—men, women, and children—who made their way to the window of her anchorhold. To be sure, these happenings affected Julian's spiritual growth and wisdom.

Norwich: The Setting

A visitor to Saint Julian's Church today will not be encouraged in any escapist illusions. The area around the church is drab. Electrical and engineering plants loom nearby, and much other evidence of contemporary industrial activity inhabits the same city block. Nonetheless, the layout of the streets and courts on either side of nearby King Street is medieval, and it is easy to visualize the clusters of houses that probably surrounded the church when Julian lived there.

Another link between Julian's time and today is the magnificent stone keep, or central fortress, of Norwich Castle, which remains as a splendid example of Norman military architecture.

The Norwich cathedral is also much as it was when Julian was alive. Considerable improvements were made on it during the fourteenth century, and stirring events of the time are recorded within it. The beautiful ornamental screen behind the altar was donated in thanksgiving to God by Bishop Henry, whose swift military initiative put down the Peasants' Revolt. A huge arch erected outside the cathedral by a local lord commemorates the English victory over the French at Agincourt in 1415. It is likely that Julian heard the singing, dancing, and revelry of celebrations honoring this triumph.

Norwich was a bustling city, and Julian's spirituality was born and nurtured in the middle of it. She lived and breathed its sounds and smells through the hearts and souls of those who sought her counsel and guidance. While free from many of the world's distractions, she did not forget or ignore its existence. Through the window of her anchorhold, Julian listened to tales of the world's woes, dispensed what comfort she could, and shared God's love with those who came to her.

Julian's Work: Showings for Our Times

Soon after her showings from God, Julian wrote a short version of the revelations. Fifteen or twenty years later she produced an extended version of the same sixteen revelations. This long text is the product of much editing and rewriting by Julian. Through symbols, images, and parables, she translated her experiences into theological concepts.

Julian has been cited as the first English woman of letters and the first theologian to write originally in English. She wrote but one work, *A Book of Showings,* yet through this one work, with its subsequent revisions, she stands out as a brilliant writer, scholar, theologian, and spiritual guide.

In contrast to women visionaries on the Continent—such as Mechtild of Magdeburg, Bridget of Sweden, and Catherine of Siena, who occupied positions of influence in medieval Europe—Julian was born into an England that looked with disfavor on the spiritual revelations of women. She protested against this convention: "Because I am a woman ought I therefore to believe that I should not tell you of the goodness of God, when I saw at the same time that it is his will that it be known?" (*Showings,* p. 135). Julian simply recorded her revelations, prepared for by faith and held in faith. No mention of preliminary ascetical exercises is included in her writings other than an insistence on the necessity of "cleaving" or "clinging" to the goodness of God.

Julian's originality is as striking as her command of the Middle English in which she wrote. Scholars have stated that her book is undoubtedly the most profound and complex of all medieval spiritual writings.

Julian's Spirituality

Commentators on Julian's work seem unanimous in their opinion that Julian's most outstanding trait as a theologian was her remarkable imagination. Her employment of this gift is typified in the predominant themes of her spirituality.

Her Image of the Trinity

When Julian thought of Father, Son, and Spirit, she spoke of God as Maker, Keeper, Lover. She presented the summit of her understanding of the Trinity in this statement:

> And so I saw that God rejoices that he is our Father, and God rejoices that he is our Mother, and God rejoices that he is our true spouse, and that our soul is his beloved wife. (*Showings,* p. 279)

References to maternal and feminine images of God (such as Isaiah 66:13, "As a mother comforts a child, so I shall comfort you") appear periodically in the Bible. In other writings, maternal terminology in reference to God has a history of usage from the time of the early leaders of the Christian Church. Clement of Alexandria, for example, wrote of the "Father's loving breasts."

What makes Julian's contribution to our image of the Trinity original is the theological precision with which she applied father-mother symbolism to the Trinitarian interrelationships. In Julian's understanding of the Trinity, fatherhood meant power and goodness, and motherhood meant wisdom and lovingness. She presented the motherhood of God as a complement to God's fatherhood.

Julian concentrated on Jesus' nurturing and teaching roles. She identified Jesus with those persons whom she described in functional terms as "mother." Here are some of her words about Jesus' relationship to us:

> But our true Mother Jesus, he alone bears us for joy and for endless life, blessed may he be. So he carries us within him in love. . . . The mother can give her child to suck of her milk, but our precious Mother Jesus can feed us with himself, and does, most courteously and most tenderly, with the blessed sacrament, which is the precious food of true life. (*Showings,* p. 298)

Her Optimism

Obsession with sin, damnation, and death permeated medieval life. One can imagine how pilgrims welcomed Julian's emphasis on God's goodness, love, and mercy. For years she struggled with a seeming inconsistency between her experience of God's unconditional love and the teachings of the Church on God's judgment, final damnation, and salvation. Astonishingly, Julian avowed her complete belief in all teachings of Mother Church while diligently pursuing her own understanding of the apparent conflict.

Julian worked out a theology of sin and salvation that was faithful to her own experience of God. Throughout this process, God comforted her that all would be well:

> And so our good Lord answered all the questions and doubts which I could raise, saying most comfortingly: I may make all things well, and I can make all things well, and I shall make all things well, and I will make all things well; and you will see yourself that every kind of thing will be well. (*Showings,* p. 229)

God's Unbounded Love for All Creation

In fourteenth-century theology, the worth of the created world was downplayed. Yet, ample evidence in Julian's text explains her understanding of the ultimate worth of Creation in the eyes of God. She recorded this insight with these words:

> And in this [the Lord] showed me something small, no bigger than a hazelnut, lying in the palm of my hand, as it seemed to me, and it was as round as a ball. I looked at it with the eye of my understanding and thought: What can this be? . . .
>
> In this little thing I saw three properties. The first is that God made it, the second is that God loves it, the third is that God preserves it. But what did I see in it? God is the Creator and the protector and the lover. (*Showings,* p. 183)

In Julian's spirituality, every human person had ultimate significance. Indeed, Creation itself had ultimate worth.

Grounded in God's Word

Julian's *Showings* demonstrates both originality and personal insight, which are astonishing accomplishments, considering her limited formal education. In her development of the shorter version of *Showings* into the final version, Julian gave us a wonderful example of her journey from deep faith to deeper faith coupled with profound understanding.

Although few facts about Julian of Norwich's life have been documented, one fact is apparent: *Showings* is a book permeated with biblical spirituality, particularly that of the Christian Testament. The writings of Saint John and Saint Paul are regularly echoed in Julian's revelations. But even though her thoughts and writings mirror biblical spirituality, she rarely quoted from the Bible. Julian was so absorbed in the revelations of God that she felt free to speak of those revelations in terms of her own personality and understanding.

However, three Johannine passages can serve as a summary of Julian's teaching on the love of God:

> For this is how God loved the world:
> he gave his only Son,
> so that everyone who believes in him may not perish
> but may have eternal life.
> For God sent his Son into the world
> not to judge the world,
> but so that through him the world might be saved.
>
> (John 3:16–17)

> Now sentence is being passed on this world;
> now the prince of this world is to be driven out.
> And when I am lifted up from the earth,
> I shall draw all people to myself.
>
> (John 12:31–32)

> We have recognised for ourselves,
> and put our faith in, the love God has for us.
> God is love,
> and whoever remains in love remains in God
> and God in him.
> Love comes to its perfection in us
> when we can face the Day of Judgement fearlessly,
> because even in this world
> we have become as he is.
>
> (1 John 4:16–17)

These passages from John illustrate Julian's own vision of a loving Christ who will make all of Creation new. The love of Christ is being poured out to all people even now.

Like Saint Paul, Julian saw the oneness of humanity in Adam and the oneness of restored humanity in Jesus. One of Julian's constant themes is that God desires for all people to be saved; her tenth showing from God emphasized that God's delight "is in your holiness and in your endless joy and bliss in me" (*Showings*, p. 221).

In describing her revelations, Julian did not get lost in the physical aspects of the Crucifixion. Rather, the Passion of Jesus that was revealed to Julian was central to her understanding of Jesus' plan for our salvation. Saint Paul was determined "that the only knowledge I would have . . . was

knowledge of Jesus, and of him as the crucified Christ" (1 Corinthians 2:2), and from that perspective he expounded the
whole mystery of Christ in creation, redemption, and trans-
figuration of all things. Julian did likewise.

Julian for Today

With her warmth and understanding, Julian can help us re-
new our inner vision. Although advances in technology and
science have been multiplying at astonishing rates, true wisdom and sympathetic understanding of the things of human
life often seem glaringly absent.

Julian shows us how God can be loved here in this place
and now in this time. By the richness of her writing, with its
mingling of earth and heaven, of what is of body and of spirit, she shows us that it is only in and through the light of God
that we can ever fully appreciate or enjoy the world that God
has made and our own life within it.

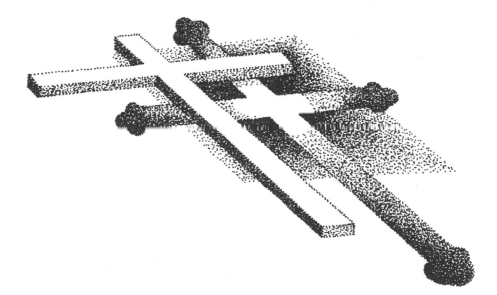

✧ Meditation 1 ✧

God Is Our Mother

Theme: Julian of Norwich experienced dramatic revelations from God. One of her special realizations was that God is our Mother, who gives us life.

Opening prayer: God, you know my heart and thoughts, and you lead me in the way that is everlasting.

About Julian

In *Showings*, Julian introduces herself to us as one who is commissioned to share her grace and wisdom with everyone who is interested:

> Here is a vision shown by the goodness of God to a devout woman, and her name is Julian, who is a recluse at Norwich and still alive, A.D. 1413, in which vision are very many words of comfort, greatly moving for all those who desire to be Christ's lovers. (*Showings*, p. 125)

Nearly two hundred pages later, Julian ends her account of God's revelations by reasserting that her showings came from Jesus:

> Our Lord very humbly revealed words to me, without voice and without opening of lips, just as he had done before, and said very sweetly: Know it well, it was no

hallucination which you saw today, but accept and believe it and hold firmly to it, and comfort yourself with it and trust in it, and you will not be overcome. These last words were said to me to teach me perfect certainty that it is our Lord Jesus who revealed everything to me. (*Showings*, pp. 314–315)

Central to the revelations is the idea that God is infinitely more than a single image of God as Father; God is also our Mother who comforts us and in whom we can have absolute trust.

Pause: Reflect on the image of God as our Mother.

Julian's Words

And so in our making, God almighty is our loving Father, and God all wisdom is our loving Mother, with the love and the goodness of the Holy Spirit, which is all one God, one Lord. . . .

. . . For he is our Mother, brother and saviour; and in our good Lord the Holy Spirit we have our reward and our gift for our living and our labour, endlessly surpassing all that we desire in his marvelous courtesy, out of his great plentiful grace. For all our life consists of three: In the first we have our being, and in the second we have our increasing, and in the third we have our fulfillment. This first is nature, the second is mercy, and the third is grace.

As to the first, I saw and understood that the high might of the Trinity is our Father, and the deep wisdom of the Trinity is our Mother, and the great love of the Trinity is our Lord; and all these we have in nature and in our substantial creation. . . .

Thus in our Father, God almighty, we have our being, and in our Mother of mercy we have our reforming and restoring, in whom our parts are united and all made perfect man, and through the rewards and the gifts of grace of the Holy Spirit we are fulfilled. (*Showings,* pp. 293–295)

Reflection

Julian addresses the most basic of religious questions, Who is God? Although Julian was not the first to use female imagery in reference to God, she is notable for the theological precision with which she explores the richness of female metaphors for God. Here she helps us to understand the deeper reality of this imagery; she is not telling us that God is like our mother but rather that our mother is like God:

> God, our Mother, is
> Wisdom
> Mercy
> Reforming
> Restoring
> In whom our parts are united
>   and all made perfect.

Life is lived in the three moments of being, increasing, and fulfilling. Just as the Trinity is one, these three aspects of our life move like a spiral that is deepening and widening at the same time, or as Julian said in Middle English, "forth spredying."

One benefit of imaging God as our Mother is that the wisdom, mercy, reforming, and restoring given by our Mother unify and perfect us as we deepen and widen, as we spread forth in God's love.

In our earliest religious lessons we learned that God made us: from God's love we received our being. How we are to respond to that love is something we spend the rest of our life learning. Julian is wonderful in what she teaches us about this "forth spredying," this increasing.

✧ Reflect for a time on the image of God as our Mother filled with wisdom and mercy, reforming and restoring us. Are you comfortable with this image? Does this image offer you a new way of experiencing God's love?

✧ How have you shared your wisdom and mercy recently? Bring to mind and heart some of the ways in which you have been a wise counselor and merciful mother to people in the last week or so.

✧ Think about some ways in which you have increased in your own love for God. Compare your love for God today with what it was when you were a child. Thank God now for this increasing in your life.

✧ Pray for awareness of how you can help someone else think of God's love as being like a mother's love—someone in your family, a friend who is distressed, a neighbor who is lonely, a co-worker who is harried, or someone else who is in need of love and loving.

✧ If you keep a journal, write a letter to God our Mother discussing an area of your life in which you need to be restored and renewed. Or write your reactions to this meditation about God as our Mother.

God's Word

Rejoice with Jerusalem,
be glad for her, all you who love her!
Rejoice, rejoice with her,
all you who mourned her!

So that you may be suckled and satisfied
from her consoling breast,
so that you may drink deep with delight
from her generous nipple.

For Yahweh says this:
Look, I am going to send peace
flowing over her like a river,
and like a stream in spate
the glory of the nations.

You will be suckled, carried on her hip
and fondled in her lap.
As a mother comforts a child,
so I shall comfort you;
you will be comforted in Jerusalem.

(Isaiah 66:10–13)

Jerusalem, Jerusalem . . . How often I have longed to gather your children together, as a hen gathers her chicks under her wings! . . . (Matthew 23:37)

Closing prayer: God, our Mother, through your ever-present grace, may my hopes and efforts be fulfilled.

✧ Meditation 2 ✧

Why We Should Pray

Theme: God is the goodness in all of life. We can never exhaust God's love for us.

Opening prayer: God, you receive our prayer as incense and our uplifted heart as a sacrifice. You are present here and now.

About Julian

In the play *Julian*, by J. Janda, the holy woman celebrates the goodness of God—the wellspring for our prayers.

Listen.

Birds sing.

Cedar and shrub
gleam
with raindrops.

There is a freshness
in the air

and a quickness
in these old bones. . . .

. . . .

(*She puts her hand out to feel the rain.*)

Everything is being
bathed, washed—

you can hear the rain
splashing off the eaves,

the fat drops are the
size of herring scales,

there is a smell
of wet earth
in the cool air,

a mother robin
is nested
in the hawthorn,

(*She leans out window to better see the robin.*)

she is brooding
with
wings spread
over the
nest,

rain rolls off
her wings,

she is warming
the new life,
the shelled promise.

"God is all that is good,
as to my sight,
and the goodness
that everything hath,
it is he."

And the Christ,
he came to make
all things new,

and his death,
it was for love:

the cruel scourging,
the mocking,
the hurtful crowning—

for love.

It runs plenteously
as
rain off the eaves

(*She holds out her hands, catching the rain, and then splashes the water on her face gently. She then beholds the water in her hands as if it had become the blood of Christ.*)

splashing, bathing,
washing, increasing

all life that is—

this rain becoming
all that it loves and
keeps in its making

the blood of Christ—

beyond our wit
the
force of its flowing
its
never beginning
its
never ending

with promise of
springs
fresh full and
flowering
as sea froth the
blossoming

(*She stares at her hands and slowly extends them outwards.*)

must be our dying
must be our dying.

(*Julian*, p. 46–49)

Pause: Reflect on the goodness of God.

Julian's Words

Prayer unites the soul to God. . . . Prayer is a witness that the soul wills as God wills, and it eases the conscience and fits man for grace. And so he teaches us to pray and to have firm trust that we shall have it; for he beholds us in love, and wants to make us partners in his good will and work. And so he moves us to pray for what it pleases him to do, and for this prayer and good desire which come to us by his gift he will repay us. . . .

. . . The whole reason why we pray is to be united into the vision and contemplation of him to whom we pray, wonderfully rejoicing with reverent fear, and with so much sweetness and delight in him that we cannot pray at all except as he moves us at the time. (*Showings*, pp. 253–254)

Reflection

In many places in her showings, Julian discussed why we should pray. She realized that most often we offer many reasons for God to grant our prayer, such as because of the holy Passion and death of Jesus. Or we beseech God to hear us for the love of Mary or for a particular saint. Although all prayers please God, the loftiest prayer, Julian says, is to God for God's own goodness. Indeed, even with the other reasons we might use, it pleases God that we recognize that God is the goodness in all of them. So we may ask God all that we will because we can never exhaust God's love for us or for our needs. God's goodness, she tells us, is closer to us than our clothing is to our body; God beholds us in love.

Why should we pray? We pray to God to be united with God's will and work. God's will and work is love.

✧ Recall your reasons for praying. What do you usually pray about?

✧ Read the section "About Julian" again. Then close your eyes and let your imagination experience birds singing, raindrops glistening on cedar and shrub, rain splashing off the eaves, the smell of wet earth. Relish in your imagination the scene she paints.

✧ If you are near a window (preferably an open window), look out and sense what is there. Take it all in. Then repeat this prayer slowly, over and over again: "God is all that is good."

✧ How is God good to you? In your own words, thank God for some of the things you have just realized are graces to you.

✧ Is there anything you can do today to help someone else experience God's goodness? Be concrete.

✧ If you keep a journal, write a dialog between you and Jesus, discussing how you can stay more closely in touch with all that is good.

God's Word

I love you, Yahweh, because you have heard
my voice and my supplications,
because you have inclined your ear to me.
Therefore I will call on you as long as I live. . . .

What return can I make to Yahweh
for all your goodness to me?
I will take up the cup of salvation,
invoking the name of Yahweh.

I will pay what I vowed to Yahweh.
May the whole nation be present! . . .

I will offer you the thanksgiving sacrifice,
invoking your name, Yahweh.

I will fulfill what I vowed to you
in the presence of all the people
in the courts of the house of Yahweh,
in your midst, Jerusalem.

(Psalm 116:1–2,12–14,17–19)

Closing prayer: O God, keep me aware of all goodness
throughout this day.

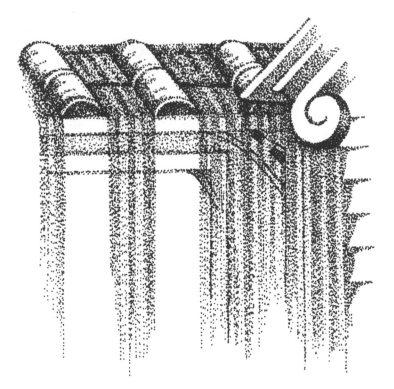

✧ Meditation 3 ✧

True Spirituality

Theme: True spirituality is the fruit of compassion and contemplation.

Opening prayer: God, you are compassionate in forgiving all of my offenses, redeeming my life from destruction, and crowning me with love. I am mindful of your presence, O God of compassion.

About Julian

Although most of Julian's original anchorhold was destroyed when the church was bombed during World War II, the anchorhold has been rebuilt on its original site.

Julian's anchorhold seems to have been a room about ten feet square, and it may have had a small patch of garden outside. It had an internal window through which Julian could see the high altar of the church. Thus she could take part in services and meditate upon the Blessed Sacrament reserved there.

A second window looked out directly onto a road that, in those days, was right beside the church. Consequently, Julian could not have totally ignored the sights and sounds of the world rushing by even if she had wanted to avoid them. Evidently, many visitors stopped at that window to speak with her and to ask for her prayers and help.

The third means of access to her room was a door or per-haps a third window, primarily for communication with her serving-woman. From a will dictated during her lifetime by a citizen of Norwich, it has been learned that Julian had at least two servants, Sara and Alice, who shopped and transacted necessary business for her. A stained-glass window in Nor-wich Cathedral depicts her with a cat, but there is no other evidence that she owned one. Anchoresses were discouraged from keeping most animals because of the distractions occa-sioned in caring for them. Cats, however—being semi-inde-pendent—were regarded as appropriate pets, so it is possible that Julian had the company of a cat in her anchorhold.

Pause: Take a moment now to visualize Julian's anchor-hold.

Julian's Words

God is everything which is good, as I see, and the good-ness which everything has is God.

God showed me this in the first vision, and he gave me space and time to contemplate it. And then the bodi-ly vision ceased, and the spiritual vision persisted in my understanding. And I waited with reverent fear, rejoicing in what I saw and wishing, as much as I dared, to see more, if that were God's will, or to see the same vision for a longer time.

In all this I was greatly moved in love towards my fellow Christians, that they might all see and know the same as I saw, for I wished it to be a comfort to them, for all this vision was shown for all men. (*Showings*, p. 190)

Reflection

Even though Julian was confined to her anchorhold, she knew that spirituality could never be a purely personal quest for peace and inner harmony. True spirituality is intimately involved in the anguish of the world. This involvement is rooted in the Incarnation of Jesus the Christ, who took on human flesh and blood and involved himself in the lives of ordinary people.

We can learn from Julian that spirituality must be earthy, caring, compassionate, involved, and committed. Such a spirituality is the fruit of true contemplation. Julian's anchorhold was a place where compassion and contemplation met.

Through the window into the church, Julian contemplated the mysteries of the faith epitomized in the Holy Eucharist and the action of the liturgy. Through the windows into the room of her maidservant and onto the street, Julian contemplated the Body of Christ in its daily human form. Through her counsel to travelers and townsfolk, she let the fruits of her contemplation spill over in compassion for her sister and brother Christians.

✧ After Jesus revealed his great love for Julian, she was "greatly moved in love towards [other] Christians," and she "wished it to be a comfort to them." Bring to mind some moments when you have been greatly moved in love toward other people and have been a comfort to them. Close your eyes, relax, breathe deeply, and explore your memories of times when the love that God has given to you moved you, in turn, to show love toward other Christians. Reflect on those moments of grace.

✧ Select the one line from "Julian's Words" that most touched you. Read it over several times, letting it inspire and inflame your heart and mind.

✧ Have you ever resented people for interfering with your desire to be alone to pray, even though they genuinely needed your help? Can you recall a particular example? How did you respond? How do you feel about it now?

✧ True spirituality requires some time for getting away. Think of at least one way that you can refresh your spirit or replenish your own "well" today.

✧ One of the most simple but effective prayers for busy people is only one line long: "Lord Jesus Christ, have mercy on me." Repeat this traditional prayer often today, just to celebrate the presence of Jesus. Say it in your own words if you prefer.

✧ In your journal, write a dialog between the part of you that wants more time for quiet prayer and the part of you that is called to active love. See if the two parts can become better friends.

God's Word

Though I command languages both human and angelic— if I speak without love, I am no more than a gong booming or a cymbal clashing. And though I have the power of prophecy, to penetrate all mysteries and knowledge, and though I have all the faith necessary to move mountains—if I am without love, I am nothing. Though I should give away to the poor all that I possess, and even give up my body to be burned—if I am without love, it will do me no good whatever.

Love is always patient and kind; love is never jealous; love is not boastful or conceited; it is never rude and never seeks its own advantage; it does not take offence or store up grievances. Love does not rejoice at wrongdoing, but finds its joy in truth. It is always ready to make allowances, to trust, to hope and to endure whatever comes.

Love never comes to an end. (1 Corinthians 13:1–7)

Closing prayer: God, teach me patience with all the demands put upon my spirit. Grant me the grace that will keep my well from running dry.

✧ Meditation 4 ✧

We Are Fastened on God

Theme: Out of love, God created all things. Thus only when we are substantially united to God can we ever be truly happy.

Opening prayer: I remember your presence, God of Love. I know that only in you can I experience lasting peace and complete joy.

About Julian

The following poem, "Mother Julian," praises God for showing Julian that all of Creation—even such an inconsequential object as a hazelnut—was created, is loved, and is preserved by God.

Mother Julian

A little thing you showed her, the size of a hazelnut;
    On the palm of her hand, round like a ball it lay.
"What is it," she said, "this little fragile thing?"
    "It is all that is made," you said, "and exists now and forever
        for I love it."

This little fragile thing, all that is made—
    Thousands of millions of galaxies, billions of billions of stars
    whirling in immeasurable space, limitless-seeming,
        incomprehensible;
    vast, unimaginably vast: brain-whirling, mind-numbing
    (yet sparkling in simple beauty on mountain lake)
        because you love it all.

These little things—
    Microscopic Diatomaceae, primal sea plants:
    fifteen thousand intricate designs, infinitesimally small
    designs, maintained through millions of years:
        such beauty for earth's basic food!
        such lavish waste, such prodigality!
           because you love earth so.

These fragile things—
    Strange animal creatures, two-footed furless mammals;
    slow-developing creatures, born vulnerable and weak;
    large-brained, mind-filled creatures: flesh and spirit
        hunting, hurting, hating; longing, laughing, loving:
        knowing (though not knowing) that you love them.

This little fragile thing—
    Final creature of them all, cell and primate recapitulating;
    burning, blissful Love, condensed to human measure:
    babe in manger laid: length, breadth, height, and depth
    of stars and cells and souls encompassing:
        such beauty for earth's heavenly food!
        such lavish prodigality for humankind and in it all,
           because you love it all!

                                  (Barbara Bishop)

Pause: Reflect on the wonders of God's Creation.

Julian's Words

And in this he showed me something small, no bigger than a hazelnut, lying in the palm of my hand, as it seemed to me, and it was as round as a ball. I looked at it with the eye of my understanding and thought: What can this be? I was amazed that it could last, for I thought that because of its littleness it would suddenly have fallen into nothing. And I was answered in my understanding: It lasts and always will, because God loves it; and thus everything has being through the love of God.

In this little thing I saw three properties. The first is that God made it, the second is that God loves it, the third is that God preserves it. But what did I see in it? It is that God is the Creator and the protector and the lover. For until I am substantially united to him, I can never have perfect rest or true happiness, until, that is, I am so attached to him that there can be no created thing between my God and me. (*Showings,* p. 183)

Reflection

In her words we can see that Julian learned two lessons that gave foundation to her growth in hopefulness.

First, she gained insight into the awesome power of God the Creator, whose hands hold the entire universe. Even though all of Creation appears to be insignificant in comparison to God's power, God loves and cares for it. God is its Maker, Keeper, and Lover. Julian realized that God especially loves and cares for people.

Secondly, Julian saw that she needed to rely on God to achieve what she was unable to achieve through her efforts alone. She understood that God loves us and helps us not because we are good but because God is good.

The image of the hazelnut is one of Julian's earliest showings, and it is the foundation of her subsequent writings. Here Julian suggests that we should be hopeful, not so that we can be fulfilled but so that we can commit ourselves to an unshakable belief in God in the uncontrollable aspects of our life now as well as in an unknown future. As the late theologian Karl Rahner wrote, God is the future that sustains us.

Julian's writings echo the words of Saint Paul to the Romans: "May the God of hope fill you with all joy and peace in your faith, so that in the power of the Holy Spirit you may be rich in hope" (Romans 15:13). Christian hope is a gift, but to make it real in our life, we must accept it.

✧ Do you ever lose hope? What causes you to lose hope? Anxiety? Exhaustion? Failure? Physical suffering? In your mind or in your journal, describe one or two times when you lost hope. Then, ask yourself why you had become temporarily unfastened from God.

✧ What things or events are signs of hope for you? Write your own list of reasons for being hopeful. Then pray your list as a litany with the refrain "I hope in you, O God" or a similar phrase. For example:
+ Because of each new day's morning light,
  I hope in you, O God.
+ Because of spring's bringing new life to earth,
  I hope in you, O God.
+ Because of smiling children's trust,
  I hope in you, O God.
Keep this list, add to it as days pass, and pray your litany, especially when you need to be reminded of God's intimate care for you.

✧ Buy some hazelnuts with their shells still on (chestnuts or even acorns will do if you cannot find hazelnuts). Let these be a reminder of Julian's showing. As you occasionally handle one of them or glance at them on your desk, table, or chest of drawers, think about what the hazelnut teaches you about life. Let it be a symbol of spiritual nourishment for you. Share Julian's story of the hazelnut with someone.

✧ Various lines in the sections "About Julian" and "Julian's Words" offer solace. Choose one comforting line and use it as a prayer.

God's Word

O God, our God,
how glorious is your name over all the earth!

Your glory is praised in the heavens.
Out of the mouths of children and babes
you have fashioned praise because of your foes,
to silence the enemy and the rebellious.

When I look at your heavens, the work of your hands,
the moon and the stars which you created—
who are we that you should be mindful of us,
that you should care for us?

You have made us little less than the gods
and crowned us with glory and honor.
You have given us rule over the works of your hands,
putting all things under our feet:

all sheep and oxen,
yes, and the beasts of the field;
the birds of the air, the fishes of the sea,
and whatever swims the paths of the seas.

God, our God,
how glorious is your name over all the earth!

(Psalm 8:1–9)

Closing prayer: O God of Love, everything has being through your love. Amen. Alleluia!

✧ **Meditation 5** ✧

God Alone Suffices

Theme: God is love. God is eternal. Only God satisfies the longings of the human spirit.

Opening prayer: O God, open my lips, and my mouth shall proclaim your praise.

About Julian

Although separated by language, culture, and tradition, Julian of Norwich and Teresa of Ávila shared the conviction that only God suffices.

Julian

God, of your goodness,
give me yourself,
for you are enough for me, and
I can ask for nothing . . . less
which can pay you full worship.
And if I ask for anything . . . less
always I am in want;
but only in you do I have everything.
(*Showings*, p.184)

Teresa

Let nothing disturb you,
nothing cause you fear;
All things pass
God is unchanging.
Patience obtains all:
Whoever has God
Needs nothing else,
God alone suffices.
(*Saints for All Seasons*, p.128)

The prayer of Teresa of Ávila cited above is familiar to many people today. This sixteenth-century Spanish-born Carmelite nun lived and wrote during the Counter-Reformation in Spain, under the shadow of the Inquisition. So, like Julian, she lived in a period of political unrest. But she had a different temperament than Julian did. Teresa was more directly involved in social affairs than Julian was, and she was interested in civil law as well as church law. Teresa's mission—the founding of strict and enclosed monasteries—satisfied her longing to be actively involved in reforming religious life.

Once she began her work, Teresa had to deal with critics, disciples, and worldly concerns. She was in a leadership position—strong and determined enough to endure riding back and forth over country roads on the back of a mule in all kinds of weather. In contrast to Julian, Teresa spent many of her later years outside the enclosure of her monasteries.

However much Julian and Teresa were different in externals, each grasped the fact that in having God she had everything else. The leap of faith that affirmed this fact for each of them was born out in their personal experience—God alone suffices.

Pause: Pray the prayers of Julian and Teresa.

Julian's Words

As truly as God is our Father, so truly is God our Mother, and he revealed that in everything, and especially in these sweet words where he says: I am he; that is to say: I am he, the power and goodness of fatherhood; I am he, the wisdom and the lovingness of motherhood; I am he, the light and the grace which is all blessed love; I am he, the Trinity; I am he, the unity; I am he, the great supreme goodness of every kind of thing; I am he who makes you to love; I am he who makes you to long; I am he, the endless fulfilling of all true desires. (*Showings*, pp. 295–296)

Reflection

Julian's phrase "you are enough for me" is echoed in Teresa's famous words, "God alone suffices." These words capture the basis of their spirituality, and both women were convinced that all Christians should share in this insight. All Christians share in the life of the Church, the sacraments, and the Gospel, and these are fully sufficient places in which to meet God, according to Julian and Teresa.

Both women focused on Jesus the Christ, who is our companion throughout our life, and both saw this companionship nourished by prayer and compassion for their neighbors. For Julian and Teresa, the real effect of prayer was measured by its fruitfulness in their life. They were never merely speculative about their experiences; they continually recognized practical applications for them in ordinary life. They challenged us to do likewise.

Julian and Teresa saw that God is enough. Their aim— through their writings—was to help us believe this and act on it. Then we shall know this truth for ourselves: God alone suffices.

✧ Spend a little time in stillness. If anything is causing you to be anxious or doubtful, try to let it go, if only for a few moments. To symbolize this release of worry and doubt, open your hands, palms up, on your lap. Feel the calm. Then focus on the words of Julian and Teresa given in the section "About Julian." Pray the words slowly. Resolve to recall these words throughout the day, especially if you realize you are becoming anxious.

✧ All too often, advertisements tell us that we need this or that to be fully alive, to be all that we can be. We might infer from some ads that on the bottom line, God is not only insufficient but not even in the picture. Do you experience any pressure to put your faith in things instead of in God? Has anything blinded you from seeing that ultimately we are dependent on God's love?

✧ Recall someone you know who is troubled. Pray for him or her.

✧ God showed Julian that Yahweh is "the endless fulfilling of all true desires." Relax in the presence of God our loving Mother. Bring to mind some of the times when your true desires were fulfilled or when "the light and the grace" or "blessed love" was given to you. Close your eyes and rest your body to contemplate the sufficiency of God.

✧ In your journal, write your reflections on Julian's statement, "God, of your goodness, give me yourself, for you are enough for me."

God's Word

Blessed be God the Father of our Lord Jesus Christ, who in his great mercy has given us a new birth into a living hope through the resurrection of Jesus Christ from the dead and into a heritage that can never be spoilt or soiled and never fade away. It is reserved in heaven for you who are being kept safe by God's power through faith until the salvation which has been prepared is revealed at the final point of time. (1 Peter 1:3–5)

Closing prayer: End your meditation by thoughtfully praying Psalm 138:

Thank you, Yahweh, with all my heart,
I sing praise to you before the angels.

I worship at your holy temple and praise your name
because of your constant love and faithfulness,
because you have shown that you and your word are
    exalted.

You answered me when I called to you;
you built up strength within me.

All the rulers of the earth will praise you, Yahweh,
because they have heard your promises.

They will sing about your ways
and about your great glory.

Even though you are exalted,
you care for the lowly.
The proud cannot hide from you.

Even when I am surrounded by troubles,
you keep me safe;
you oppose my angry enemies
and save me by your power.

You will do everything you have promised me;
Yahweh, your faithful love endures forever.
Complete the work that you have begun.

✧ **Meditation 6** ✧

We All Need to Be Loved and to Love

Theme: Joy and peace come to us only when we are content with God and when we are loving and content with ourselves and other Christians. God loves us and works to bring us peace.

Opening prayer: O my God, "you have always been my help, and in the shadow of your wings I rejoice" (Psalm 63:7). In your presence, I listen to your Spirit.

About Julian

In the play *Julian*, John Ball's mother comes to Julian, seeking comfort because her son (a priest and revolutionary leader) has been hanged, drawn, and quartered. Julian takes her in and lets her stay until her spirit calms. Of Mrs. Ball's healing, we hear Julian say:

> Then one day she looked
> out that window,
> turned and said,
>
> "Dame Julian,
> I must leave your nest,
> I feel I can fly."

I helped her
gather her few
belongings,

a new shift
she had made

and a warm wool cloak
I did not need.

(*Julian walks the woman to the door USR, opens it; they embrace.*)

"Lady Julian,
you are the first
creature
that ever loved me,"
said she, then left.

(*Julian closes door.*)

She never came again.

The kind priest
that brought her
to me—returned again.

He told me she was
now roaming the streets
of London—begging,

crying, "Peace,
peace to all,"

and though many
thought she had lost
her wits,

I knew that
she had found
her soul—

and that,
none could take
from her—
or ever remove.

(Janda, *Julian*, pp. 98–99)

Pause: Reflect on the healing power of love.

Julian's Words

We cannot be blessedly saved until we are truly in peace and in love, for that is our salvation.

. . . We are sure and safe by God's merciful protection, so that we do not perish. But we are not blessedly safe, possessing our endless joy, until we are all in peace and in love, that is today wholly contented with God and with all his works and with all his judgments, and loving and content with ourselves and with our fellow Christians and with everything which God loves, as is pleasing to love. And God's goodness does this in us.

So I saw that God is our true peace; and he is our safe protector when we ourselves are in disquiet, and he constantly works to bring us into endless peace. (*Showings*, pp. 264–265)

Reflection

God accepts us as we are and loves us, even when we are in need of forgiveness. The realization that God never ceases to love us is a deep source of peace. The love and peace within us overflow to other Christians and to "everything which God loves." Compassion is an act of flowing over toward another.

Peace does not come from simply isolating one's self from the troubles and suffering of others; we are expected to bear one another's burdens, just as Julian integrated her personal interior life with the social aspect of Christianity. Jesus does not reveal his love just to make us feel good but so that the peace and love given to us can overflow to other people through compassion.

✧ Select the one line from "Julian's Words" that most touches you. Pray it over and over again, relishing its meaning and consolation.

✧ One useful definition of love is as follows: seeking and then fostering the best for others in their concrete situations. Julian fostered the good of John Ball's mother first by taking her in when she was desperate and then by sending her forth knowing that she was loved. Using the following descriptions of self-love, nurturing love, and friendship as guides, meditate unhurriedly on those you love and those who love you. (You may want to write your responses.)

✦ *Self-love:* Julian, imitating Jesus, wanted us to be "loving and content with ourselves." List all the ways that you demonstrate love for yourself. Then dialog with Jesus about ways in which you might love yourself more fully.

✦ *Nurturing love:* This type of love fosters the good of those who may be unable to help themselves, such as children, poor or homeless people, and those who are ill. List instances in which you nurtured other people last week. Meditate on each situation; let the face of each person come to mind. Then recall instances when you were nurtured by other people last week. List them.

Offer a prayer of thanksgiving for each person who has shown you nurturing love.

✦ *Friendship:* This type of love is characterized by mutual caring and usually involves loyalty, support, and a shared view of the world. Friends help each other to achieve what is good. Now remember all of your friends. Spend some time just visualizing their face and recalling the sound of their voice. Relish each friend. Pick one friend with whom you have not been in contact recently; resolve to call, write, or visit him or her soon. Offer into God's loving care the name of each friend.

✧ *The Ancrene Rule,* a manual drawn up for people who led a solitary life, was written more than a hundred years before Julian was born. She followed this "Rule," so it gives us a clue to Julian's life of prayer. To enter into the spirit of Julian's prayer life and to reflect on Jesus' love for us, try this repetitive prayer from the "Devotions" section of the manual:

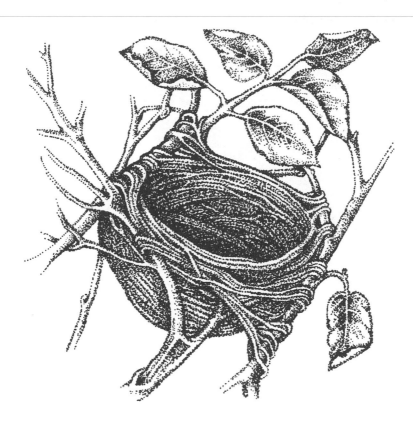

Jesus Christ, Son of the Living God,
have mercy on us.

Thou who didst condescend to be born of a virgin,
have mercy on us.

Solitaries prayed these words each morning after dressing
and frequently at other times. Repeat the prayer from time to
time today.

✧ Recall some people who desperately need God's peace. Pray a litany for them, alternating responses. For example:

✦ For what we have done to children of war,
Jesus Christ, Son of the Living God,
have mercy on us!

✦ For our indifference to hungry and homeless people,
Thou who didst condescend to be born of a virgin,
have mercy on us!

Then add personal petitions such as these:

✦ For my own hesitation to comfort others,
Jesus Christ, Son of the Living God,
have mercy on me!

✦ For my failure to take time to see the needs of others,
Thou who didst condescend to be born of a virgin,
have mercy on me!

God's Word

Always be joyful, then, in the Lord; I repeat, be joyful. Let your good sense be obvious to everybody. The Lord is near. Never worry about anything; but tell God all your desires of every kind in prayer and petition shot through with gratitude, and the peace of God which is beyond our understanding will guard your hearts and your thoughts in Christ Jesus. (Philippians 4:4–7)

Closing prayer: O my God, give me the strength to be loving to everyone in need whom I meet today.

✧ Meditation 7 ✧

Nothing Can Separate Us from God's Love

Theme: Despite our sinfulness, nothing can interfere with God's love for us.

Opening prayer: God, you are all goodness, present now.

About Julian

In Janda's play, Julian shares her thoughts about how God treats us:

> Crocuses—can you see them?
> And a clump of snowdrops? so delicate.
>
> It comes so gently,
> spring,
> that's how God touches us,
> so gently,
> as spring—or as a father,
> a father with his firstborn.
>
> The mother knows no fear
> in picking up the child
> and nursing it,

but the father,
he is afraid.
He must be coaxed
to do it.

God our Father loves us
full tenderly
as a firstborn—

at times,
I think he
is afraid of us.

(*She crosses to bed and puts her book down, and then looks through window above bed.*)

Sometimes,
I cannot sit still
at sermon time:

one would think
the priest had the holy oils
poured on him
to preach hate.

God does not hate,
God cannot hate,
God will not hate,
what he has made.

(Janda, *Julian*, pp. 73–74)

Pause: Reflect on the last stanza; repeat it several times.

Julian's Words

And so in all this contemplation it seemed to me that it was necessary to see and to know that we are sinners and commit many evil deeds which we ought to forsake, and leave many good deeds undone which we ought to do, so that we deserve pain, blame and wrath. And despite all this, I saw truly that our Lord was never angry, and never will be. Because he is God, he is good, he is truth, he is love, he is peace; and his power, his wisdom, his charity and his unity do not allow him to be angry.

For I saw truly that it is against the property of his power to be angry, and against the property of his wisdom and against the property of his goodness. God is that goodness which cannot be angry, for God is nothing but goodness. Our soul is united to him who is unchangeable goodness. And between God and our soul there is neither wrath nor forgiveness in his sight. For our soul is so wholly united to God, through his own goodness, that between God and our soul nothing can interpose. (*Showings*, p. 259)

Reflection

When we are confronted with our sins and failures, we might imagine an angry God who seeks to have us change our ways out of fear of God's reprisal. Julian was undoubtedly aware of the presence of this rather common notion in medieval religious thinking. Yet in all of her showings Julian, amazingly, never represented God as being angry. Steeped in the Scriptures as she was, Julian was able to uncover the sometimes hidden view of God's gentle love.

Julian was firm in her conviction that God desires us to renounce our sins—like brushing away the dead leaves of winter to let the budding crocuses feel the sun. As the words of Ezekiel assure us, God takes no pleasure in punishing anyone (Ezekiel 18:21–32).

Perhaps our limited understanding of God's gentle love is a reflection of our own reluctance to forgive others—or ourselves. That is, we tend to form an image of God in our own likeness.

Julian's imaging of God as Mother can be helpful here, for it reminds us that God as Father gives us redemption from sins and that God as Mother gives us life itself. God's love—like parental love—wills life and, when life comes into being, exclaims, "It is good that you exist!" Then parental love nurtures what it has brought into existence, desiring growth and fulfillment despite the child's failings. No human love can be perfectly just and impartial, but Julian wants us to realize that nothing can separate us from God's love.

✧ What is there in your life that requires God's forgiveness? Once you have named this, lift it up to God like incense rising to the sky.

✧ Do you find some things especially difficult to forgive in others? List all of these on paper or in your journal. Then close your eyes. Concentrate on breathing in a slow, relaxed way. Relax your body. Let all tensions go. Imagine yourself in a forest glade or near a waterfall or beside the sea—someplace where you feel calm, open, and relaxed. Next, imagine that Jesus comes to be with you, saying, "Peace be with you, my friend." You want to tell him about how hard it is to forgive certain people for offenses against you. Seeing Jesus' willingness to listen, you talk to him. Talk to Jesus as long as you need to. When you have finished talking, Jesus says, "Let us pray the prayer that I taught the disciples to say. Our Father . . ." At last, Jesus embraces you, and then he walks softly away.

✧ Spend some time reflecting on the one person who has hurt you most deeply. Bring this person to mind; hear the words that passed between you; recall the hurt. Write a description of the hurtful incident. Then offer the hurt up to God. Slowly and deliberately tear up (into small pieces) the paper on which you described your hurt. Let the anger and pain go, the release being a gift to God, who wishes us to be free of hate and bitterness.

✧ Ask God for a gentle heart that will be tolerant of others and forgive those who have grievously wounded you.

God's Word

So then, now that we have been justified by faith, we are at peace with God through our Lord Jesus Christ; it is through him by faith, that we have been admitted into God's favour in which we are living, and look forward exultantly to God's. . . . The love of God has been poured into our hearts by the Holy Spirit which has been given to us. (Romans 5:1–2,5)

Closing prayer: Begin your closing prayer with a moment of silence, holding in your heart the feelings of hope that come from knowing that God's forgiving mercy can never be exhausted. Then pray using Julian's words:

God does not hate,
God cannot hate,
God will not hate,
what he has made.

Courage

Theme: We should have courage because our faithful God will not let us be overcome by the powers of evil.

Opening prayer: Keep me, O God, as the apple of your eye, and may my eyes be fixed on you.

About Julian

When Julian was an old and revered woman, she was visited by the much-traveled Margery Kempe of Kings Lynne. The visit took place in 1413 when Margery, herself a devout woman, sought Julian's advice because she had heard that Julian "was expert in such things, and good counsel could give" (*The Book of Margery Kempe*, p. 33).

Margery was a colorful woman who, in many respects, was as different from Julian as can be imagined. Julian lived as a solitary attached to the church of Saint Julian at Norwich, whereas Margery was a married woman and a mother (of fourteen children) who traveled throughout England and to places as distant as Jerusalem and Rome. Margery was a center of controversy for most of her adult life because of her boisterous sobbing in response to church sermons, services, and sacraments, particularly the Eucharist. She was quite unlike the contemplative Julian, whose life and demeanor were marked by peace and quiet.

Margery's account of her conversation with Julian appears in chapter 18 of the first part of *The Book of Margery Kempe*. This talk is the only glimpse we have of Julian in action, as seen by another person, and it gives us a sense of her reputation. Margery wrote:

> Then she was bidden by Our Lord to go to an anchoress in the same city [Norwich], named Dame [Julian], and so she did, and showed her the grace that God put into her soul, of compunction, contrition, sweetness and devotion, compassion with holy meditation and high contemplation, and full many holy speeches and dalliance that Our Lord spake to her soul; and many wonderful revelations, which she shewed to the anchoress to find out if there were any deceit in them, for the anchoress was expert in such things, and good counsel could give.
>
> The anchoress, hearing the marvellous goodness of Our Lord, highly thanked God with all her heart for His visitation, counselling this creature to be obedient to the will of Our Lord God and to fulfill with all her might whatever He put into her soul, if it were not against the worship of God, and profit of her fellow Christians. (P. 33)

Margery's account of her visit confirms the impression of Julian that can be derived from *Showings*. For instance, Julian's emphasis on the love of God, in her revelations, is echoed in her advice to Margery: "The Holy Ghost moveth ne'er a thing against charity, for if He did, He would be contrary to His own self for He is all charity" (*Kempe*, p. 34).

The other teachings recorded by Margery in her account closely agree with those present in Julian's writings. Evidently Margery had found a soul-friend in Julian and was able to reflect back on what they exchanged as sisters in spirit.

Pause: Ponder Julian's advice to Margery.

Julian's Words

By contrition we are made clean, by compassion we are made ready, and by true longing for God we are made worthy. These are three means, as I understand, through which all souls come to heaven, those, that is to say, who have been sinners on earth and will be saved. . . .

. . . For our courteous Lord does not want his servants to despair because they fall often and grievously; for our falling does not hinder him in loving us. Peace and love are always in us, living and working, but we are not always in peace and in love; but he wants us so to take heed that he is the foundation of our whole life in love, and furthermore that he is our everlasting protector, and mightily defends us against all our enemies. (*Showings*, p. 245)

Just so [our Lord] said in the last words with perfect fidelity, alluding to us all: You will not be overcome. And all this teaching and this true strengthening apply generally to all my fellow Christians, as is said before, and so is the will of God.

And these words: you will not be overcome, were said very insistently and strongly, for certainty and strength against every tribulation which may come. He did not say: You will not be troubled, you will not be belaboured, you will not be disquieted; but he said: You will not be overcome. (*Showings*, p. 315)

Reflection

"Julian's Words" help us to understand Margery Kempe's enthusiasm for the wisdom of Julian's spiritual guidance. Indeed, throughout *Showings* Julian was concerned about helping others to grow in their spiritual life. Yet she did not want to draw attention to herself. She wanted to be transparent—a medium through which God's graces could be revealed to all of her "fellow Christians." Julian was careful to explain the plain meaning of what had been shown to her, for her own benefit and for that of her readers.

Julian's recounting of her showings was a process of unfolding meaning and insight, and she did so with great care, intelligence, and imagination. Like Margery, we too can draw courage from Julian's words.

✧ Slowly reread the last paragraph of "Julian's Words," letting the meaning touch your heart and mind. Select one phrase, such as "You will not be overcome," and repeat it as a prayer.

✧ Reflect on the sources of stress and anxiety in your life. (You may want to commit your reflections to paper.) Try to name all of them; be as exacting as possible. Then answer these questions for each source of stress: Is this an important matter? If it is, should I be worried even though God assures me that I will not be overcome? Lastly, raise up these worries and fearful specters, asking God to soothe your soul with peace.

✧ Imagine that you are a traveler who is seeking Julian's counsel about an issue that has been a great trial for you. See yourself approaching Julian's window, knocking softly, and then being confronted by the face of Julian. Tell Julian your troubles, and listen to her counsel. (If you think it might be helpful, write the conversation.)

✧ Offer some words of trust and hope in God. Praying a litany may be helpful. For example:
✦ In all my anxious moments, O God,
   I know I shall not be overcome.
✦ In all my fears, O God,
   I shall not be overcome.
✦ In all my attempts at peacemaking, O God,
   I shall not be overcome.
✦ In a world in which there is so much suffering,
   you will overcome, O God.
✦ In a world of dying hopes,
   you will overcome, O God.

✦ In the tears of oppressed people,
   you will overcome, O God.
(Continue with a litany of your own concerns, petitions, and praise.)

God's Word

Can anything cut us off from the love of Christ—can hardships or distress, or persecution, or lack of food and clothing, or threats or violence; . . . No; we come through all these things triumphantly victorious, by the power of him who loved us. For I am certain of this: neither death nor life, nor angels, nor principalities, nothing already in existence and nothing still to come, nor any power, nor the heights nor the depths, nor any created thing whatever, will be able to come between us and the love of God, known to us in Christ Jesus our Lord. (Romans 8:35,37–39)

Closing prayer: End your meditation by prayerfully reaffirming Julian's words:

I know that at times I will be troubled,
I know that at times I will be belaboured,
I know that at times I will be disquieted,
but I believe that I will not be overcome.
Amen.

✧ **Meditation 9** ✧

Trust in Our Giftedness

Theme: God wants us to trust in our own giftedness. After all, these gifts come from our Creator.

Opening prayer: O God, you have called us to share your glory. You are present to me now.

About Julian

In her memoirs, Margery Kempe provided a tantalizing glimpse of Julian the wise counselor. Julian was wise because she depended on the revelations given to her by God, and she fully believed that God is all goodness, love, and truth. Julian's advice to Margery stands in sharp contrast to the initial treatment given Margery when she consulted Richard of Caistor, parish priest of Saint Stephen's Church, Norwich.

Margery Kempe visited Richard of Caistor with the express purpose of "praying him that she might speak with him an hour or else two hours at afternoon, when he had eaten, in the love of God" (*Kempe*, p. 30). Kempe reported that the priest, reputed for his holiness, replied: "'Benedicite. How could a woman occupy an hour or two hours in the love of Our Lord? I shall never eat meat till I learn what ye can say of Our Lord God in the time of an hour'" (p. 30).

Reflected in this passage is the stereotypical view of women that was prevalent in Julian's time. Not only did such

narrow views of women prevail in society; they also domi-
nated the thinking of religious leaders. Julian would have
been familiar with narrow views about the nature and poten-
tial of women as reflected in the writings of major Christian
theologians such as Augustine, Jerome, and Thomas Aquinas.

Richard of Caistor overcame his immediate reaction to
Margery. Indeed, she said of him:

> "Notwithstanding the rumours and the grutching of the
> people against her, this holy man . . . whom God hath
> exalted, and through marvellous works shewn and
> proved for holy, ever held with her and supported her
> against her enemies, unto his power, after the time that
> she, by the bidding of God, had shewn him her manner
> of governance and living, for he trustfully believed that
> she was well learned in the law of God." (Pp. 31–32)

Given the restrictions placed on women, even on the ex-
pressions of their spirituality, it is amazing that Julian was
able to rise above her society's prejudices. No trace of restrict-
ed views concerning the spiritual life of women is found in
any of the showings that Julian recorded. Julian's revelations
survive because of the spiritual richness that they manifest.
Julian trusted that God could work through her despite the
thinking of the society of her time. God gave her the revelations and, along with them, the gift to share them with other
people.

Pause: Reflect on God's gifts to you.

Julian's Words

But God forbid that you should say or assume that I am
a teacher, for that is not and never was my intention; for
I am a woman, ignorant, weak and frail. But I know very
well that what I am saying I have received by the revela-
tion of him who is the sovereign teacher. But it is truly
love which moves me to tell it to you, for I want God to
be known and my fellow Christians to prosper, as I hope
to prosper myself, by hating sin more and loving God
more. But because I am a woman, ought I therefore to
believe that I should not tell you of the goodness of God,

when I saw at that same time that it is his will that it be known? You will see this clearly in what follows, if it be well and truly accepted. Then will you soon forget me who am a wretch, and do this, so that I am no hindrance to you, and you will contemplate Jesus. (*Showings,* p. 135)

Reflection

How easy it is to put people in boxes! How often we label people when we speak of them or think of them. Such stereotyping often puts limits on how people respond when they become aware of our limited view of them. Knowing the narrow roles assigned the women of her time, Julian might well have hidden her revelations or never have written her *Showings.*

Just as we can put people into boxes, we can help pull them out. This is well-documented in psychologists' studies of what has come to be known as the "Pygmalion effect," a label for what happens to people when much is expected of them. The Broadway musical *My Fair Lady,* which was based on George Bernard Shaw's play *Pygmalion,* popularized the concept of the Pygmalion effect. In the story, a street urchin, Eliza Doolittle, becomes a "lady" because she is treated as a lady. As the play ends, she affirms herself as competent, intelligent, and articulate. But first, she had to be treated as a lady by other people.

The feast of the Incarnation, Christmas, reminds us that God expects us to become holy, and we believe that it is possible because one who is like us—Jesus the Christ, our exemplar—has gone before us to show us that it is so. Because Julian followed Jesus' example, she is a model for us. She overcame her own hesitancy, which was born of the narrow view of women that permeated her time. In so doing, Julian trusted that her faithfulness to God would help lead others to learn from God as well. God calls all humans, women and men, to "be filled with the utter fullness of God" (Ephesians 3:21) and to "keep their minds constantly occupied in doing good works" (Titus 3:8).

✧ Write fifteen sentences about yourself, each beginning with "I am . . ." and concluding with acknowledgment of a God-given gift of personality or character.

✧ Write "I can" fifteen times in a column, skipping a line after each phrase. Then quickly complete the statements. For example, "I can relax with most people and listen to them."

✧ Using your "I am" and "I can" lists, compose a litany of gifts for which you are grateful, for example, "For the gift of making close friends, I thank and praise you, O God!" Pray your litany slowly and meditatively.

✧ Ask for God's strength in overcoming whatever keeps you from doing what you know in your heart needs to be done—either in your family, at work, in your circle of friends, or in the human family.

✧ Recall an instance in which you felt put down by someone. Let all the details come back to your consciousness. Pray that God's grace will heal the hurt feelings that might arise in that memory.

✧ Pray for the wisdom to recognize anything in your heart or mind that limits other people in any way. Pray also for the strength to overcome it.

God's Word

Each one of you has received a special grace, so, like good stewards responsible for all these varied graces of God, put it at the service of others. If anyone is a speaker, let it be as the words of God, if anyone serves, let it be as in strength granted by God; so that in everything God may receive the glory, through Jesus Christ, since to him alone belong all glory and power for ever and ever. Amen. (1 Peter 4:10–11)

Closing prayer: Complete your meditation with a prayerful reading of these words from the Psalms:

> Yahweh, you search me and know me.
> You know if I am standing or sitting.
>
> . . . .
>
> You created my inmost being
> and knit me together in my mother's womb.
> For all these mysteries—
> for the wonder of myself,
> for the wonder of your works—
> I thank you.
>
> (Psalm 139:1,13–14)

✧ Meditation 10 ✧

Recognizing Goodness

Theme: Those who are filled with light see the good, even in darkness.

Opening prayer: In your light, O God, I see light. Your light is shining upon me now.

About Julian

Thomas Merton, perhaps the most universally admired spiritual writer of the twentieth century, wrote:

> Julian [of Norwich] is without doubt one of the most wonderful of all Christian voices. She gets greater and greater in my eyes as I grow older and whereas in the old days I used to be crazy about St. John of the Cross, I would not exchange him now for Julian if you gave me the world and the Indies and all the Spanish mystics rolled up in one bundle. I think that Julian of Norwich is with Newman the greatest English theologian. She is really that. For she reasons from her experience of the substantial center of the great Christian mystery of Redemption. She gives her experience and her deductions, clearly, separating the two. And the experience is of course nothing merely subjective. It is the objective mystery of Christ as apprehended by her, with the mind and formation of a fourteenth century English woman. And

that fourteenth century England is to me and always has been a world of light. (*Seeds of Destruction*, pp. 274–275)

Pause: Ponder the last two sentences from Thomas Merton.

Julian's Words

Our faith is a light, coming in nature from our endless day, which is our Father, God; in which light our Mother, Christ, and our good Lord the Holy Spirit lead us in this passing life. This light is measured with discretion, and it is present to us in our need in the night. The light is the cause of our life, the night is the cause of our pain and all our woe, in which woe we deserve endless reward and thanks from God; for we by his mercy and grace willingly know and believe our light, walking therein wisely and mightily. And at the end of woe, suddenly our eyes will be opened, and in the clearness of our sight our light will be full, which light is God, our Creator, Father, and the Holy Spirit, in Christ Jesus our saviour.

So I saw and understood that our faith is our light in our night, which light is God, our endless day. (*Showings*, p. 340)

Reflection

We need spiritual sight in order to see through the darkness of evil and suffering. Both Julian and Thomas Merton lived in times when darkness was real but in which the light of faith gave hope. They knew the darkness of war and all of its accompanying confusion and horror.

In the midst of the Peasants' Revolt, Julian was a beacon of light to those who sought her counsel. She still could hope that light would conquer the darkness of suffering. Thomas

Merton lived during World War II, the Korean War, and a prolonged war in Vietnam—clashes that were far more devastating than those Julian knew.

That Merton found light for his faith in a woman of fourteenth-century England is remarkable. For Merton, Julian illuminated the power of Christ's redemption without trivializing human pain and suffering. Her insight makes redemption real in present experience.

We need redemption today. The dark cloud of war looms more ominously than when Thomas Merton was alive—so great is our capacity to inflict destruction. Yet we still have the chance to choose the light of life. With Julian, Thomas Merton, and all who would be peacemakers we can draw hope from these words of Jesus the Christ: "I am the light of the world; anyone who follows me will not be walking in the dark but will have the light of life" (John 8:12).

✧ What is your experience of darkness? Bring to mind several sources of darkness that block out joy, hope—light—for you. The sources of darkness may be both interior and exterior. (God knows these dark areas already; this meditation is intended to help you name your dark areas in order to discover God's illumination.)

✧ Now recall times of light, times when you experienced joy and hope, love and compassion. Bring Jesus to mind; he is ever present if we would only acknowledge his being with us. See Jesus as light. Talk to him about your darkness, listen to his response, and ask him to lift you out of the darkness. (You may find that writing the dialog is helpful because at another time of darkness, you can add to your written dialog with Jesus.)

✧ Light a candle, then dwell a few moments on the peace that comes with believing that—like the sun in the morning sky—the Savior of the world will come. Then all Creation shall see the saving power of God—possibly in your own lifetime, perhaps even today! Reflect on the wonderful light that makes crops grow, that makes the rough places smooth, that warms us. When you are ready, move into the next stage of your meditation on the light.

✧ With your candle lit, sit comfortably—hands on your lap, feet planted firmly on Mother Earth. Close your eyes. Breathe slowly, concentrating on your breath. Relax. Let all tensions go. Let your body unwind. Rest in the presence of the Light—God, Jesus, Spirit. Begin repeating a one-word prayer, "Light." Slowly say the word over and over. If a distraction inserts itself, do not be bothered. Just repeat your prayer, "Light." Rest and be illumined by God's light.

✧ Think of two ways, perhaps small, through which you can be a light in the world today. How can you bring the peace and light of Jesus into your world?

God's Word

Sin speaks to sinners
in the depths of their hearts.
No awe of God is before their eyes.

They so flatter themselves
that they do not know their guilt.

In their mouths are lies and foolishness.
Gone is all wisdom.

They plot the downfall of goodness
as they lie on their beds.
They set their feet on evil ways,
they hold to what is evil.

Your love, Yahweh, reaches to heaven;
your faithfulness to the skies.

Your justice is like a mountain—
your judgments like the deep.
To all creation you give protection.

Your people find refuge
in the shelter of your wings.

They feast on the riches of your house;
they drink from the stream of your delight.

You are the source of life,
and in your light we see light.

Continue your love to those who know you,
doing justice to the upright in heart.

Let the foot of the proud not crush me,
nor the hand of the wicked drive me away.

See how the evildoers have fallen!
Flung down, they shall never rise.

(Psalm 36)

Closing prayer: O God, increase in me the faith that "is our light in our night, which light is God, our endless day."

✧ **Meditation 11** ✧

Compassion

Theme: Jesus showed the greatest compassion for humankind. We too are called to a life of compassion.

Opening prayer: May your love be upon me, O God, for I put my hope in you.

About Julian

Julian could not have remained unaffected by the social and political upheavals taking place in and around Norwich. Writing about Julian, Kenneth Leech says the following about one of her contemporaries:

> Now there was in East Anglia at the same time as Julian another Christian figure of whom we know little: a priest called John Ball. John Ball was one of the leaders of the Peasants' Revolt of 1381 when the rural poor, industrial workers, and a significant number of the lower clergy revolted against the harsh taxation laws, and demanded the ending of serfdom—and, incidentally, of hierarchy within the Church and clergy. (They chopped off the head of the Archbishop of Canterbury, Simon of Sudbury, and his head can still be seen in the local church of Sudbury in Suffolk!) "I have come not from heaven but from Essex," announced John Ball. Ball was a hedge priest, a *sacerdos vagans*, a wanderer, and it is therefore

open to speculation that his journeyings in East Anglia might have led him beyond his home city of Colchester to Norwich, and to Julian's cell.

What might have happened had the contemplative of Norwich and the radical priest of Essex met? What would they have said to each other, these early representatives of contemplative solitude and liberation theology? What would have been the common ground between the mystic and the militant? (*Julian: Woman of Our Day*, p. 92)

What would the two of them, Julian and John, say if they could speak to us today?

Pause: Bring to mind persons who have sought justice for poor and oppressed people in recent years.

Julian's Words

The mother may sometimes suffer the child to fall and to be distressed in various ways, for its own benefit, but she can never suffer any kind of peril to come to her child, because of her love. And though our earthly mother may suffer her child to perish, our heavenly Mother Jesus may never suffer us who are his children to perish, for he is almighty, all wisdom and all love, and so is none but he, blessed may he be. . . .

And if we do not then feel ourselves eased, let us at once be sure that he is behaving as a wise Mother. For if he sees that it is profitable to us to mourn and to weep, with compassion and pity he suffers that until the right time has come, out of his love. . . .

It is his office to save us, it is his glory to do it, and it is his will that we know it; for he wants us to love him sweetly and trust in him meekly and greatly. And he revealed this in these gracious words: I protect you very safely. (*Showings*, pp. 300–302)

Reflection

Compassion and contemplation should never be at odds with each other. Spirituality must not be simply a quest for personal peace and inner harmony. True spirituality is intimately involved in the anguish of the world, for it is rooted in the Incarnation and Passion of Christ.

Without prayer or mysticism, politics can become cruel and barbaric. Without action or works, love, prayer, and mysticism soon become sentimental or uncommitted interiority. In an inseparable two-in-oneness, Christian faith thus has both mystical and action-oriented dimensions. The bond between the two is laid by the ethical dimension of Christian faith—an especially important insight for our times.

In the words of the theologian Gustavo Gutiérrez, "we drink from our own wells." Our own spirituality is inextricably bound with our acts of compassion and our work for justice.

Julian's writing leaves no room for the privatism of much of our present-day religious culture. Jesus shared a vision of Christians creating a peaceable kingdom, a loving community, and the conditions that make it possible for all of God's children to be fully alive. Julian carried a vision that held promise in the midst of pain. We are called to be carriers of a new vision and of the legacy of hope that we have inherited through people like Julian.

We have been saved by God's compassion, by Jesus becoming flesh and blood, dying and rising for us, and by the loving, constant presence of the Spirit. It is Jesus' "office to save us." It is our office to be Jesus' compassion now.

✧ Pick up today's newspaper. Flip through the pages and notice headlines that herald events of human tragedy, events that call for Jesus' compassion. Then in the same newspaper, find articles that show the peaceable kingdom being created, a loving community existing, or people being fully alive. Pray for those who are suffering and give thanks for those who are fulfilling Jesus' vision.

✧ Julian noted that sometimes Jesus "sees that it is profitable to us to mourn and to weep, with compassion and pity he suffers that until the right time has come, out of his love." Recall a time in **your life** when suffering taught you a valuable lesson or when your own pain and sorrow helped you become more compassionate to other people. If this has not happened yet, think of a present suffering. How can this suffering be a source of empathy for other people who are suffering?

✧ Lift up to God, who protects us "very safely," the names of people you know who are suffering now. Ask God for the strength to build the peaceable kingdom, a loving community, and a world where all of God's children can be fully alive.

God's Word

Blessed be the God and Father of our Lord Jesus Christ, the merciful Father and the God who gives every possible encouragement; he supports us in every hardship, so that we are able to come to the support of others, in every hardship of theirs because of the encouragement that we ourselves receive from God. For just as the sufferings of Christ overflow into our lives; so too does the encouragement we receive through Christ. So if we have hardships to undergo, this will contribute to your encouragement and your salvation; if we receive encouragement, this is to gain for you the encouragement which enables you to bear with perseverance the same sufferings as we do. So our hope for you is secure in the knowledge that you share the encouragement we receive, no less than the sufferings we bear. (2 Corinthians 1:3–7)

Closing prayer: End your meditation with this traditional prayer:

Come, Holy Spirit,
fill the hearts of your people.
Kindle in us the fire of your love.
Send forth your spirit,
and we shall be created.
And you shall restore the face of the earth.
Amen.

We Are God's Work of Art

Theme: "We are God's work of art" (Ephesians 2:10). Thus, we should rejoice in our bodiliness.

Opening prayer: Let me drink from the river of delight, O God, and rejoice now in your presence.

About Julian

What makes Julian real and alive for us today? Perhaps she is so vivid because early in her writings we are confronted with a Julian of flesh, blood, and spirit. She was a woman who was at home with her body, and her spirituality reflected this integration.

In one of her earliest showings, Julian realized that God overcomes all evil. This insight released such glad emotion in her that she "laughed greatly." She wrote that her laughter was so contagious that all of those around her began to laugh as well, even though they had gathered because they thought that she was dying. Julian went on to say that their laughter was pleasing to her and that she wished all Christians could have seen what she saw so that they could have laughed with her.

Julian understood that we may laugh to comfort ourselves and to rejoice with God. Laughter is essential to the body and soul, for we are embodied people, and God comes to us in our body and our soul. According to Julian, our senses are holy. God wills that creatures enjoy life. In *Showings*, Julian encourages us to do all in our power to preserve our consolation. She reminds us that bliss lasts forever but pain is passing.

In her own words, "It is not God's will that when we feel pain we should pursue it in sorrow and mourning for it, but that suddenly we should pass it over, and preserve ourselves in the endless delight which is God" (*Showings*, p. 205). Julian believed that the proper end of our senses is pleasure, not pain.

Pause: Enjoy the sounds, smells, touch, and sight of the life around you.

Julian's Words

And when our soul is breathed into our body, at which time we are made sensual, at once mercy and grace begin to work, having care of us and protecting us with pity and love, in which operation the Holy Spirit forms in our faith the hope that we shall return up above to our substance, into the power of Christ, increased and fulfilled through the Holy Spirit. So I understood that our sensuality is founded in nature, in mercy and in grace, and this foundation enables us to receive gifts which lead us to endless life. For I saw very surely that our substance is in God, and I also saw that God is in our sensuality, for in the same instant and place in which our soul is made sensual, in that same instant and place exists the city of God, ordained for him from without beginning. He comes into this city and will never depart from it, for God is never out of the soul, in which he will dwell blessedly without end. (*Showings*, pp. 286–287)

Reflection

We should enjoy our experience of God. The love of God does not require a life of weak, spiritless subservience to God, to individuals, or to institutions. Nor does love of God require the negation of our senses. In Julian's spirituality, our substance and sensuality together may rightly be called our soul, and our experience of God can be expressed in our physical senses: "We shall all be endlessly hidden in God, truly seeing and wholly feeling, and hearing him spiritually and delectably smelling him and sweetly tasting him" (*Showings*, p. 255). Spirituality requires that we care for our body as well as our spirit.

What does this imply? At least that we do nothing that is obviously harmful to our body and that we do all we can to cherish this temple of the Holy Spirit. Adequate rest, a nourishing diet, routine exercise, and management of stress are essential to a healthy body and spirit. Much medical evidence shows a link between health of body and that of spirit.

Many great mystics in the Christian tradition as well as in Eastern religions have recognized the link between body and spirit. Fasting, yoga, dance, gesturing, and prayer postures reflect the deep weavings of body and spirit in our journey toward the Center whom we call God.

The object of caring for our body and our spirit is to become strengthened, energized, and empowered to care for others—our neighbors here and throughout the world. But loving the body and soul of other people means that we first love our own body and soul. We are a work of God's art. Indeed, we are created in God's own image (Genesis 1:26).

✧ Read "Julian's Words" again. Select a line that touches you. Repeat the line several times to appreciate its meaning.

✧ At some point in life, most of us look at ourself in the mirror and say something like, "I'm five-four, a short guy, but I am lovable and I can love others," or "I'm six-three, tall for a woman, but I am lovable and I can love others." List and describe aspects of your body that you like and aspects that you would change if you could. For each characteristic write down one or more experiences (such as hearing people's comments) that have caused you to like or dislike that personal feature, for example, "Graceful hands—Uncle Mike told me that I have the hands of an artist."

Now, perhaps standing in front of a mirror, create a litany of these aspects and pray your litany to the God who created you in the Creator's image:

✦ I have many wrinkles from the years;
   I am lovable and I can love others.
✦ I have graceful hands;
   I am lovable and I can love others.

Make a habit of affirming your body and soul in this fashion as a way of giving praise to your Creator.

✧ Meditate by letting your senses become fully alive:

✦ *Sight:* From where you are sitting, feast your eyes on everything in the place where you are praying. Are not even the simplest things miracles from God's creative power?
✦ *Hearing:* Now close your eyes and listen carefully to each sound. Visualize the sources of the sounds. Spend some time listening. Then stop your ears. Imagine a world devoid of hearing.
✦ *Smell:* With your eyes shut, smell the odors around you. Recall some of your favorite fragrances: maybe garlic or a perfume or the pungent fragrance of pines after a rain. Or go into the kitchen and smell spices, foods, and so on. Smell your skin.
✦ *Touch:* Run your fingers through your hair and over your arms. Then touch objects in the room. Reflect on all the ways your sense of touch brings you delight and protects you too.
✦ *Taste:* Close your eyes and let your tongue imagine one of your favorite foods or drinks. God gave us our tongue so that we can relish the food that sustains our life.

✧ Contemplate the knuckles on your right hand. (This may sound silly until you realize what a miracle your hand is.) Wiggle your fingers and then knot your hand into a fist. Imagine those knuckles working—the tendons stretching, the

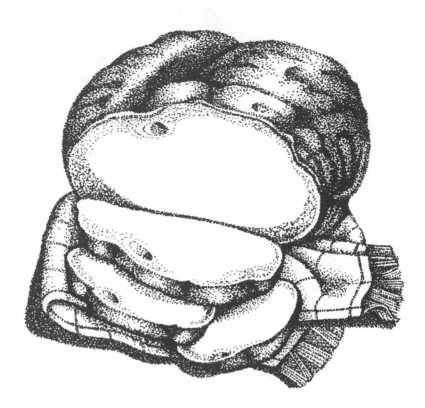

cartilage protecting the bones and preventing friction, the nerves sending messages from the brain to tell the hand to move, and the skin stretching and wrinkling to cover the knuckles. Even though scientists have become increasingly adept at making artificial joints, few professionals—if any—would boast that their products are better or more perfectly designed than your knuckles.

Contemplate the workings of some other part of your body—perhaps a part that you take for granted even though it is faithfully functioning for you moment after moment.

✧ One story about Saint Francis of Assisi relates that on his deathbed he apologized to his body for all the wrong that he had inflicted upon it. Is there anything you should apologize to your own body for? Too little sleep? Too much physical work and strain? Poor nutrition? Overeating? Overdrinking? Ignoring illness? If so, resolve to overcome your failure to cherish your body.

✧ How can you help others to delight in God or to realize that they too are God's work of art?

God's Word

O taste and see that Yahweh is good!
Blessed are those who trust in God.
Revere Yahweh, you saints;
for there is nothing lacking to those who fear God.
The lions may grow weak and hungry,
but those who seek Yahweh shall lack nothing good.
Come, sons and daughters, listen to me.

(Psalm 34:8–11)

God created . . . male and female. . . . God saw all he had made, and indeed it was very good. (Genesis 1:27,31)

Closing prayer: My God, my Creator, please help me to better appreciate the work of your art, my own body.

✧ **Meditation 13** ✧

Hope

Theme: People who believe in Jesus have every reason to rest in the hope that he will lift us up and unite us with him.

Opening prayer: My hope is not in vain because God is ever with me.

About Julian

Learning to remain hopeful amidst the darkness of suffering is a struggle in which all of us become engaged from time to time—and it can be a bitter trial. The optimism of Julian can help us as it did Thomas Merton. In his book *Conjectures of a Guilty Bystander,* Merton wrote the following:

> I pray much to have a wise heart, and perhaps the rediscovery of Lady Julian of Norwich will help me. I took her book with me on a quiet walk among the cedars. She is a true theologian . . . she really elaborates, theologically, the content of her revelations. She first experienced, then thought, and the thoughtful deepening of experience worked it back into her life, deeper and deeper, until her whole life as a recluse at Norwich was simply a matter of getting completely saturated in the light she had received all at once, in the ["showings"], when she was about to die.

One of her most telling and central convictions is her orientation to what one might call *an eschatological secret*, the hidden dynamism which is at work already and by which "all manner of thing shall be well." This "secret," this act which the Lord keeps hidden, is really the full fruit of the Parousia [Second Coming]. It is not just that "He comes," but He comes with this secret to reveal, He comes with this final answer to all the world's anguish, this answer which is already decided, but which we cannot discover and which (since we think we have reasoned it all out anyway) we have stopped trying to discover. Actually, her life was lived in the belief in this "secret," the "great deed" that the Lord will do on the Last Day, not a deed of destruction and revenge, but of mercy and of life, all partial expectations will be exploded and *everything* will be made right. It is the great deed of "the end" which is still secret, but already fully at work in the world, in spite of all its sorrow, the great deed "ordained by our Lord from without beginning." (Pp. 191–192)

Pause: Consider your sources of hope.

Julian's Words

And so I understood that any man or woman who voluntarily chooses God in his lifetime for love, he may be sure that he is endlessly loved with an endless love which makes that grace in him. For he wants us to pay true heed to this, that we are as certain in our hope to have the bliss of heaven whilst we are here as we shall be certain of it when we are there. (*Showings*, p. 308)

Glad and merry and sweet is the blessed and lovely demeanour of our Lord towards our souls, for he saw us always living in love-longing, and he wants our souls to be gladly disposed towards him, to repay him his reward. And so I hope that by his grace he lifts up and will draw our outer disposition to the inward, and will make us all at unity with him, and each of us with others in the true, lasting joy which is Jesus. (*Showings,* pp. 318–319)

Reflection

Julian's writings are permeated with Christian hope. She experienced all of the aspects of hope in her own spiritual life: the rocklike dependability of God, the God who is always near, the God of the impossible, the God who is Father and Mother to us.

Julian was especially aware of the joyful character of hope. We can see this in the number of times that her writings discuss joy and its meanings—at least fifty-five times or approximately once every three pages! Human joy is essential to Julian's spirituality. To her, we are meant to be full of joy because our joy in God reflects the joy of the Trinity. Creation is an act of God's joy. The more faithfully and hopefully we respond to God's love in our life, the greater will be the fullness of our joy.

Was Julian ever more relevant? Her message of hope surely lightened the spirits of many in her troubled age. We probably need her message at least as much today. The threat of nuclear holocaust, the possibility of extinguishing all life forms on the planet earth, and deadly violence between warring peoples are daily reminders of the cloud of despair that hovers above us. Great faith and hope are required in order to penetrate the gloom caused by shattering events like the assassination of Gandhi, of Martin Luther King, Jr., and of Archbishop Oscar Romero. We need great faith and hope to see beyond the darkness of our personal life—our failures, weaknesses, and fears.

But gloom, fear, and anxiety are only one side of reality. The other side is that we are an Easter people. Even though suffering is real, the life, Passion, death, and Resurrection of Jesus have won for each of us the assurance that death is conquered. An Easter people has hope. Alleluia!

✧ Begin this meditation, an adaptation of John 20:1–18, by relaxing and placing yourself once again in the presence of God. The setting is the cemetery where Jesus has been entombed after his horrifying death on the cross. Earlier in the morning, you went to the tomb and, finding it empty, ran to tell Peter the terrible news. Peter and John hurried back with you.

Finding the tomb empty has plunged you into sadness. . . . Questions surge in your head: "Why did they steal his body? Haven't they already killed my beloved Jesus? How could they do this? Where is he?" . . . You stoop to look inside the tomb. . . .

Two angels in white are sitting where the body of Jesus had been. . . . They ask you, "Why are you weeping?" . . .

You reply, "They have taken my Lord away, and I don't know where they have put him." . . . While still speaking, you turn around. . . .

A man is standing nearby. . . . He says, "Why are you weeping? Who are you looking for?" . . .

You suppose him to be the gardener, and you say, "Sir, if you have taken him away, tell me where you have put him, and I will go and remove him." . . . He warmly speaks your name. . . . Your eyes are opened and your heart fills with emotion. . . . You cry, "Master!" and rush to embrace Jesus. . . .

He stops you, saying gently, "Do not cling to me, because I have not yet ascended. Go and find my brothers and sisters and tell them that I am ascending to my God and your God." . . .

You rush joyously to the disciples, shouting, "I have seen the Lord! I have seen the Lord! He is risen! He is risen!"

✧ In what areas of your life do you experience hope? List these areas of hope.

✧ Spend a few moments recalling how you have experienced the joy that comes from hope. Does anything in your life give you special joy now? How can you share that joy with other people?

✧ Are any areas of your life covered by gloom and despair? If so, list them. Then write down what Julian would advise you to do if you could talk to her about these sources of despair. You might even write a dialog with her or carry on a discussion with her in your imagination.

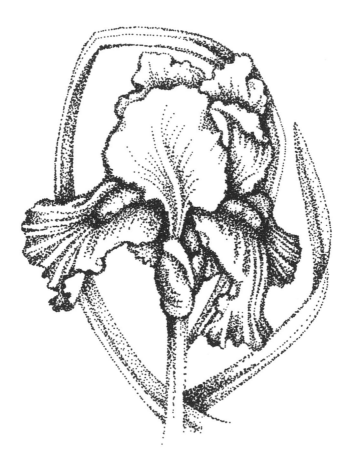

✧ To place yourself in union with Jesus, pray a litany of praise, using "Jesus, you are lasting hope" or some other short phrase from "Julian's Words" as a response.

✧ Thank and praise God for revealing the light that never fades—Jesus Christ our Savior. Ask for God's help in focusing on the hope that Julian showed us—namely, that we are "endlessly loved with an endless love." Design a poster including these words or any symbol that reminds you that you are "endlessly loved with an endless love."

God's Word

. . . As Christ was raised from the dead by the Father's glorious power, we too should begin living a new life. If we have been joined to him by dying a death like his, so we shall be by a resurrection like his. . . .

But we believe that, if we died with Christ, then we shall live with him too. We know that Christ has been raised from the dead and will never die again. Death has no power over him any more. For by dying, he is dead to sin once and for all, and now the life that he lives is life with God. In the same way, you must see yourselves as being dead to sin but alive for God in Christ Jesus. (Romans 6:4,8–11)

Closing prayer: O God, I thank you now for faith that leads to hope, which finds its fulfillment in love.

Trusting Prayer
When God Seems Absent

Theme: We live between doubt and hope, between strongly sensing God's presence and fearfully wondering whether God is absent. Julian helps us understand how our doubts and fears can be ways to God.

Opening prayer: If I listen to the words you speak to me now, you will show me the path of life, O God.

About Julian

The paradoxical experience of God's simultaneous presence and absence in our life is a recurring theme in Christian spirituality. Julian addressed this paradox at the end of her showings.

This theme can be seen also in Augustine's familiar phrase "Our hearts are restless until they rest in thee, O God." It is hauntingly explored in the words of Francis Thompson's poem "The Hound of Heaven": "I fled Him, down the nights and down the days." God is always present, but we are not always present to God. Sometimes we flee from God, but the hollow feeling in the depths of our soul propels us on our search for God.

Julian expressed the same paradox when she wrote:

For I saw him and sought him, for we are now so blind and so foolish that we can never seek God until the time when he in his goodness shows himself to us. And when by grace we see something of him, then we are moved by the same grace to seek with great desire to see him for our greater joy. So I saw him and sought him, and I had him and lacked him; and this is and should be our ordinary undertaking in this life, as I see it. (*Showings,* p. 193)

For more than fifteen years, Julian meditated on her relationship with God in order to discern what God expected of her. She did this not only for herself but for all of her "fellow Christians." She had moments of doubt, moments when God seemed to be absent. Through prayer, she tried to understand the paradox that we are called to seek God even though God is always present, always active in all of life. Julian's great trust quickly overcame her doubts.

Julian summed up God's meaning for us in her last chapter. There she explained why we seek God, who is always present. She wrote:

So I was taught that love is our Lord's meaning. . . . In this love we have our beginning, and all this shall we see in God without end.

Thanks be to God. Here ends the book of revelations of Julian the anchorite of Norwich, on whose soul may God have mercy. (*Showings,* pp. 342–343)

In moments of doubt about God's presence with us, we seek God and find love. Julian ended her book of showings by reminding us of God's steadfast love.

Pause: Reflect on moments of doubt that you may have experienced.

Julian's Words

After this our Lord revealed about prayer, in which reve-
lation I saw two conditions in our Lord's intention. One
is rightful prayer; the other is confident trust. But still
our trust is often not complete, because we are not sure
that God hears us, as we think, because of our unworthi-
ness and because we are feeling nothing at all; for often
we are as barren and dry after our prayers as we were
before. And thus when we feel so, it is our folly which is
the cause of our weakness, for I have experienced this in
myself. And our Lord brought all this suddenly to my
mind, and revealed these words and said: I am the
ground of your beseeching. First, it is my will that you
should have it, and then I make you to wish it, and then
I make you to beseech it. If you beseech it how could it
be that you would not have what you beseech? And so
in the first reason and in the three that follow, our Lord
reveals a great strengthening, as can be seen in the same
words. . . .

Our Lord is most glad and joyful because of our
prayer; and he expects it, and he wants to have it, for
with his grace it makes us like to himself in condition as
we are in nature, and such is his blessed will. For he
says: Pray wholeheartedly, though it seems to you that
this has no savour for you; still it is profitable enough,
though you may not feel that. Pray wholeheartedly,
though you may feel nothing, though you may see nothing, yes, though you think that you could not, for in dry-
ness and in barrenness, in sickness and in weakness,
then is your prayer most pleasing to me, though you
think it almost tasteless to you. And so is all your living
prayer in my sight. (*Showings,* pp. 248–249)

Reflection

Keeping a balance between doubt and hope can be tiresome.
Like Francis Thompson, we sometimes try to avoid the working of God in our life:

I fled Him, down the nights and down the days;
   I fled Him, down the arches of the years;
   I fled Him, down the labyrinthine ways
   Of my own mind; and in the midst of tears
I hid from Him, and under running laughter.

                ("The Hound of Heaven")

We might try to avoid God because we cannot control God the way we would like to—there are just too many surprises! We crave certainty, especially in our spirituality. But such a desire, in the philosopher Kierkegaard's words, can be "deceitful toward the divine."

In times of light, all spiritual pilgrims—like Augustine, Thompson, and Julian—realize that God never leaves us. We are never alone, even in our darkest moments. Julian's writings can help us realize this truth. As Thomas Merton wrote, "This is for her the heart of theology: not solving contradiction, but remaining in the midst of it, in peace. . . ." Merton went on to say that "the 'wise heart' remains in hope and in contradiction, in sorrow and in joy. . . . The wise heart lives in Christ" (*Conjectures*, p. 192).

Where does spiritual insight come from? What nourishes our strength to trust in God's presence? Julian answered this question for us: prayer. Steadfast, wholehearted prayer. We learn such prayer by praying. Even when we do not feel anything, we are in good company. We are joined with all other Christians, past and present. Even when we are not satisfied with our prayer, God finds it pleasing and worthwhile.

✧ Spend a few moments in silence, resting in God's presence. Try to focus on your inner spirit. Concentrate on your breathing. Just as your breath continues to flow, no matter what you are experiencing, so too God's love is always sustaining your spirit.

✧ When we have nagging doubts and our prayer is barren, repeating the simple but profound "Jesus prayer" may help: "Jesus Christ, Son of God, have mercy on me." If these words do not fit your mood, change them. For example: "Mother God, embrace me and my doubts." Our turning toward God—not the sophistication of the words—is the key.

❖ Offer your doubts to God. Close your eyes. Relax your body. Concentrate on slow, deep breathing. Then bring to mind all of your doubts and face them squarely in all their aspects. Talk to God about them, one by one. If you need to, argue for your doubts but—most of all—share them. Listen to God's answer, the answer within you. You may find that writing this conversation helps.

❖ Read "Julian's Words" again. If a particular phrase sticks in your mind and heart, ponder the meaning of the phrase for you. What is God telling you by drawing you to this phrase?

❖ Offer thanksgiving and praise to God for the ever-present gift of grace in your life. Lift up your heart to God.

God's Word

The Spirit too comes to help us in our weakness, for, when we do not know how to pray properly, then the Spirit personally makes our petitions for us in groans that cannot be put into words; and he who can see into all hearts knows what the Spirit means because the prayers that the Spirit makes for God's holy people are always in accordance with the mind of God. (Romans 8:26–27)

Closing prayer: End your meditation by slowly and thoughtfully repeating this traditional prayer:

Come, Holy Spirit,
fill the hearts
of your faithful
and enkindle in them
the fire of your love.
Amen.

✧ **Meditation 15** ✧

All Shall Be Well

Theme: The central message of Julian of Norwich is that all shall be well.

Opening prayer: You have restored my life, O God, and I wish to be in your presence.

About Julian

In the final scene of the play *Julian*, Julian is just finishing her meditation. She rises, comes stage front to speak with the audience once more, and says:

> Life
> is a precious thing
> to me
>
> and a little thing:
>
> my life is a little thing,
> when it will end here
> is God's secret.
>
> And the world
> is a little thing,
>
> like a hazelnut
> in his—her hand—

but it is in his ever-keeping,
it is in his ever-loving,
it is in his ever-making,

how should any thing be amiss?

Yes, all shall be well,
and all will be well,
"and thou shalt see thyself
that all manner of thing
shall be well."

Kind friends,

I pray God grant you
all your good wishes,
desires, and dreams—

it is all in the choosing,

(*She turns and starts to exit USL. She stops and smilingly turns to the audience to deliver the final line of* Julian.)

it is all in the asking.

[*So ends the play.*]

(Janda, *Julian*, pp. 105–106)

Pause: Pick one line from "About Julian" and pray it repeatedly.

Julian's Words

And so our good Lord answered to all the questions and doubts which I could raise, saying most comfortingly: I may make all things well, and I can make all things well, and I shall make all things well, and I will make all things well; and you will see yourself that every kind of thing will be well. . . .

And in these . . . words God wishes us to be enclosed in rest and in peace. (*Showings*, p. 229)

Reflection

Perhaps no other single phrase gives us a fuller taste of the multilayered riches of Julian's spirituality than does "All shall be well." This taste is enough to lure us to delve more deeply and to journey more widely into the power of Julian's mysticism.

Many people have explored the consolation and depth of Julian's spirituality. For example, the last movement of T. S. Eliot's poem *Four Quartets* links the twentieth-century poet with Dame Julian, who lived six centuries earlier:

> With the drawing of this Love and the voice of this
>   Calling
>
> We shall not cease from exploration
> And the end of all our exploring
> Will be to arrive where we started
> And we know the place for the first time.
> . . . .
> And all shall be well and
> All manner of thing shall be well. . . .

In reading about Julian's optimism, we are encouraged to see more clearly that pain is quelled by love, and we are enabled to trust in the providence of a gracious God: "It is all in the choosing, it is all in the asking." May we choose life over and over again. "All shall be well."

✧ Now that you have completed the last set of readings on Julian, take a moment to look back on what you have seen in her *Showings*. Make a list or write a summary of the most memorable lines or thoughts that have come to you during your meditations with Julian.

✧ Pray for deeper trust in God's care so that, like Julian, you will have the courage to be all that you are meant to be. Ask God to move your heart, like Julian's was moved, to seek God above all things so that you may know the peace that comes with the conviction that all shall be well.

✦ Offer some words of praise to God for the gift of Julian, who has helped you to see the wonder of God's love.

✦ Keep Julian's words in your mind and heart today. Recall them often so that they might become part of your daily, living prayer. Perhaps they can also become part of the counsel you give to those who seek your comfort and advice. As you prepare to finish your prayer time, dwell on the power of these words, letting them "rain down" on you in a shower of blessings: "All shall be well!"

God's Word

It is not ourselves that we are proclaiming, but Christ Jesus as the Lord, and ourselves as your servants for Jesus' sake. It is God who said, "Let light shine out of darkness," that has shone into our hearts to enlighten them with the knowledge of God's glory, the glory on the face of Christ.

But we hold this treasure in pots of earthenware, so that the immensity of the power is God's and not our own. (2 Corinthians 4:5–7)

Sing out your joy to the Creator, good people;
for praise is fitting for loyal hearts.

Give thanks to the Creator upon the harp,
with a ten-stringed lute sing songs.

O sing a new song;
play skillfully and loudly so all may hear.

For the word of the Creator is faithful,
and all God's works are to be trusted.

The Creator loves justice and right
and fills the earth with faithful love.

(Psalm 33:1–5)

Closing prayer: Conclude your meditation with the hymn of Mary, making the words your very own:

My being proclaims your greatness,
and my spirit finds joy in you, God my Savior.

For you have looked upon me, your servant, in my
	lowliness;
all ages to come shall call me blessed.

God, you who are mighty, have done great things for me.
Holy is your name.

Your mercy is from age to age toward those who fear
	you.

You have shown might with your arm
and confused the proud in their inmost thoughts.

You have deposed the mighty from their thrones
and raised the lowly to high places.

The hungry you have given every good thing
while the rich you have sent away empty.

You have upheld Israel your servant, ever mindful of
	your mercy—

even as you promised our ancestors;
promised Abraham, Sarah, and their descendants
	forever.

(Psalms Anew, p. 16)

Glory be to God our Creator,
to Jesus the Christ,
and to the Holy Spirit, who dwells in our midst,
both now and forever.
Amen.

·ALLELUIA·

✧ Acknowledgments ✧

The psalms quoted in this book are from *Psalms Anew: In Inclusive Language*, compiled by Nancy Schreck and Maureen Leach (Winona, MN: Saint Mary's Press, 1986). Used by permission of the publisher. All rights reserved.

All other scriptural quotations used in this book are from The New Jerusalem Bible. Copyright © 1985 by Darton, Longman & Todd, Ltd., London, and Doubleday, a division of Bantam, Doubleday, Dell Publishing Group, Inc., New York. Reprinted by permission of the publishers.

All excerpts from Julian's *Showings* are from *Julian of Norwich: Showings*, translated by Edmund Colledge and James Walsh (New York: Paulist Press, 1978). From the Classics of Western Spirituality series. Copyright © 1978 by The Missionary Society of St. Paul the Apostle in the State of New York. Used by permission of Paulist Press.

Excerpts by J. Janda on pages 29–31, 51–52, 57–58, and 99–100 are from *Julian: A Play Based on the Life of Julian of Norwich*, by Jim Janda (New York: The Seabury Press, 1984), pages 46–49, 98–99, 73–74, and 105–106 respectively. Copyright © 1984 by Jim Janda. Used by permission of Harper & Row, Publishers, Inc.

The poem on pages 40–41 is from *Julian of Norwich: Four Studies to Commemorate the Sixth Centenary of the Revelations of Divine Love*, Fairacres Publication 28 (Oxford: SLG Press, 1973), page 24. Used by permission of the author and of the publisher.

The excerpt by Teresa of Ávila on page 46 is quoted in *Saints for All Seasons*, edited by John J. Delaney (Garden City, NY: Doubleday and Co., 1978), page 128.

✧ For Further Reading ✧

Butler-Bowdon, W., trans. *The Book of Margery Kempe.* Old Greenwich, CT: Devin-Adair Company, 1944.

Del Mastro, L. *Revelations of Divine Love.* New York: Doubleday, 1977.

Enfolded in Love, translated by members of The Julian Shrine. New York: Harper and Row Publishers, Inc., 1980.

Janda, J. *Julian: A Play Based on the Life of Julian of Norwich.* New York: The Seabury Press, 1984.

Julian of Norwich: Showings, translated by Edmund Colledge and James Walsh. New York: Paulist Press, 1978.

Julian of Norwich: Four Studies to Commemorate the Sixth Centenary of the Revelations of Divine Love. Sisters of the Love of God, Fairacres Publication 28. Oxford: SLG Press, 1973.

Julian: Woman of Our Day, edited by Robert Llewelyn. Mystic, CT: Twenty-Third Publications, 1987.

Titles in the Companions for the Journey series

Praying with Julian of Norwich

Praying with Francis of Assisi

Praying with Catherine of Siena   Available spring 1990

Praying with John Baptist de La Salle   Available fall 1990

Order from

Saint Mary's Press
Terrace Heights
Winona, MN 55987-0560